Let's Read Aloud More!

音読で極める基礎英語

By
Teruhiko Kadoyama
&
Simon Capper

photographs by
iStockphoto

音声ファイルのダウンロード／ストリーミング

CD マーク表示がある箇所は、音声を弊社 HP より無料でダウンロード／ストリーミングすることができます。トップページのバナーをクリックし、書籍検索してください。書籍詳細ページに音声ダウンロードアイコンがございますのでそちらから自習用音声としてご活用ください。

https://www.seibido.co.jp

Let's Read Aloud More!

Copyright © 2015 by Teruhiko Kadoyama, Simon Capper

All rights reserved for Japan.
No part of this book may be reproduced in any form
without permission from Seibido Co., Ltd.

はしがき

　本書は、「音読」や「筆写」といった、一見地味ですが確実に英語力アップにつながる練習法を取り入れた総合英語テキストで、前作『音読で始める基礎英語』の続編に当たるものです。前作同様、基礎的な語彙や文法の確認に重点を置いていますが、オフィスを舞台にしたストーリー仕立てになっていますので、これまでの英語学習ではあまり触れる機会のなかったビジネス英語やプレゼンテーションの基礎も学ぶことができるはずです。よく言われるように、実際ビジネスの現場で使われる英語は決して難しい表現や構文ばかりではありませんから、まず本書で基本的な文法と語彙をしっかり身につけることが大切です。

　「英語を話せるようになりたい」と願う人は多いですが、授業や自宅での学習で実際にどれだけ英語を音読する練習をしてきたでしょうか？　何度も音読しなければやはり英語が口からすぐに出てくるようにはなりませんし、実際に英文を書いてみるという作業は表現を確認し定着させる上で非常に効果的です。デジタル全盛な時代にあえてこうしたアナログ的な練習方法を提唱するのは、やはり一番効果が実感しやすい方法だと思うからです。スマートフォンなどを使えば本書の付属音声をいつでもどこでも聞くことが可能ですから、音読を中心としたモバイル・ラーニングをぜひ実践してほしいと願っています。

　本書の刊行にあたっては、成美堂の佐野英一郎社長、そして編集部の工藤隆志氏に多大なご尽力を賜りました。衷心よりお礼申し上げます。

　　　　　　　　　　　　　　　　　　　　　　　　　　　　　　角山照彦　Simon Capper

このテキストの使い方

本書は 15 ユニットからなり、各ユニットの構成は次のようになっています。

WARM-UP　授業前に確認しておこう！

授業で聞く対話の中に出てくる重要単語や表現、そして文法項目を取り上げていますので、あらかじめ確認しておくと聞き取りが易しく感じられるはずです。ここは授業の予習としてやっておきましょう。

Vocabulary Preview

Grammar Point

LET'S LISTEN!　会話の大意を聞き取ろう！

オフィスを舞台にした対話やプレゼンテーションを聞いてみましょう。大意が理解できているかを試す問題が用意されています。細部まで聞き取るのは難しいですが、カンに頼るのではなく、単語レベルでよいですから正解の根拠を答えられるようにしましょう。

Question 1

Question 2

Question 3

LET'S CHECK & READ ALOUD!　音読してみよう！

空欄補充問題を設けていますので、**LET'S LISTEN!** で聞いた対話などをもう1度聞いて空欄を埋めて内容を正確に理解しましょう。内容を確認できたら、音読、そしてパートナーとロールプレイ（役割練習）をしてみましょう。

Takashi　　Rachel

Angela

GRAMMAR　文法に強くなろう！

WARM-UP で取り上げた文法項目の確認問題です。文法に苦手意識のある方はこのページでしっかり復習をしておきましょう。

LET'S READ!

異文化理解に関するパッセージやビジネスメモなどを読んでみましょう。大意が理解できているかを試す問題が用意されています。

CHALLENGE YOURSELF!

英語の資格試験としてよく知られている TOEIC® Listening & Reading Test と似た形式のリスニング問題を用意しました。試験を意識した実践的な演習をしてみましょう。

A　B　C

LET'S READ ALOUD & WRITE!　音読筆写で覚えよう！

最後に授業のまとめとして、学習した対話を音読筆写してみましょう。日本語訳だけを見ながら英文がスラスラと書けるようになることが目標です。

TABLE of CONTENTS

01 **This is my first visit there.**　スモールトーク ………………………… 8
〈現在形・過去形1〉　予定を尋ねる／別れ際の挨拶

02 **How do you like Bangkok?**　海外出張1 …………………………… 14
〈現在形・過去形2〉　挨拶する／詳細を尋ねる

03 **It's going well so far.**　海外出張2 ……………………………………… 20
〈進行形・未来形〉　礼を述べる／予定を確認する

04 **Have they decided on the design yet?**　出張報告 ……………… 26
〈現在完了形〉　経験を述べる／指示する

05 **Could you take a look at them?**　プレゼン準備1 ……………… 32
〈助動詞〉　依頼する／助言する

06 **My flight was canceled.**　電話応対 ………………………………… 38
〈受動態〉　電話での応答／説明する

07 **What do you want me to do?**　使用法説明 ……………………… 44
〈不定詞〉　意向を尋ねる／操作を説明する

08 **She knows marketing very well.**　オフィストーク1 …………… 50
〈関係詞1〉　比較する／意味を確認する

主な登場人物

サンライズ・コーポレーションの東京支店にて
営業を担当している。

タカシの同僚。

09	**Thank you for coming to our interview.** ヘッドハンティング ……… 56
	〈動名詞〉 初対面の挨拶／意見を述べる

10	**The competition will be very strong.** 会議 ……………… 62
	〈形容詞・副詞〉 意見を求める／理解を示す

11	**This is where we hold meetings.** プレゼン準備2 …………… 68
	〈関係詞2〉 案内する／提案する

12	**I'd like to talk about our latest model.** プレゼン ……………… 74
	〈分詞〉 順序を示す／重点を強調する

13	**You are much better than me.** オフィストーク2 …………… 80
	〈比較〉 感想を述べる／比較する

14	**If I were you, I wouldn't miss it.** 人事面接 ……………… 86
	〈仮定法〉 説得する／用件を尋ねる

15	**I'd like to propose a toast.** 送別会 ……………………… 92
	〈接続詞・前置詞〉 感謝する／発表する

巻末資料	品詞の分類／文の要素と基本文型／人称代名詞の種類と格変化表 音節／不規則動詞変化表／発音記号の読み方 ……………… 98

　　　リンガポルタのご紹介 ………………………………………… 103

Angela

バンコクにある取引先の社員。

Julia

サンライズ・コーポレーション東京支店の営業部長で、タカシの上司。

Carol

タカシの同僚。

UNIT 01 This is my first visit there.

文法 現在形・過去形1

タイへ出張に出かけるタカシは空港での待ち時間に、レイチェルという女性に話しかけます。会話では、予定を尋ねる表現や別れ際の挨拶を学びます。また、文法ではbe動詞（現在形・過去形）と疑問詞に焦点を当てて学習します。

WARM-UP 授業前に確認しておこう！

Vocabulary Preview

1～10の語句の意味として適切なものをa～jの中から選びましょう。 CD 02

1. excited _____
2. break _____
3. go ahead _____
4. How about...? _____
5. in charge of _____
6. business partner _____
7. have to _____
8. pleasure _____
9. I'm afraid _____
10. interesting _____

a. 休み、休憩
b. 興味深い、面白い
c. 残念ながら
d. ～しなければならない
e. 取引先
f. （命令文で）さあどうぞ
g. ワクワクして
h. 楽しみ、（仕事に対しての）娯楽
i. ～はどうですか？
j. ～の担当で

ビートに乗って1～10の語句を発音してみましょう。

Grammar Point　現在形・過去形1

I'm at the airport now. （今空港におります）
How was the trip to Singapore? （シンガポールへの旅行はどうでしたか？）

be動詞とは名詞や形容詞、場所を表す語句が後に続いて「～である、～にいる」という意味を表すもので、主語によっていろいろと形が変わります。また、「～だった、～にいた」と過去を表す場合も同じく変化します。下の表の空欄に枠の中から適切な動詞の形を選んで表を完成させましょう。

was　　am ✓　　is　　are　　were

話し手のことを1人称、相手方を2人称、それ以外の人たちを3人称と言います。

	主語		現在形	過去形
1人称	単数（私）	I	am	
	複数（私たち）	we		
2人称	単数（あなた）	you		
	複数（あなたたち）			
3人称	単数（彼、彼女、それ）	he, she, it		
	複数（彼ら、それら）	they		

「～ではない」という否定文にするときは、be 動詞のすぐ後に not をつけます。また、「～ですか？」という疑問文にするには be 動詞を主語の前に持ってきます。下の例文の日本語訳を完成させながら確認しましょう。

> is not = isn't, are not = aren't のように会話では短縮形がよく使われます。ただし、I am not は通常 I'm not となります。× I amn't

I'm sorry. Mr. Tucker <u>isn't</u> at his desk at the moment.
（_____）

<u>Is</u> this your first visit to Japan?
（_____）

なお、疑問文を作る際には、when や where などの**疑問詞**がよく使われますが、これらは通常疑問文の始めに置かれます。下の表でしっかり確認しましょう。

what	何	who	誰	how	どのように
where	どこへ（で）	why	なぜ	how far	どれくらいの距離
when	いつ	which	どれ	how long	どれくらいの時間（期間）

"<u>When</u> is the next meeting?" "On Wednesday, next week."
（「_____」「来週の水曜日です」）

"<u>How</u>'s your schedule on April 20th?" "I'm free most of the day."
（「4月20日 _____」「_____」）

be 動詞は、単に「(～は)…である」と言う場合だけでなく、《be going to...》の形で未来形、《be + -ing》の形で進行形、《be + 過去分詞》の形で受動態など、実に様々な表現で使われますので、使い方の基本をしっかりと確認しておきましょう。

LET'S LISTEN! 会話の大意を聞き取ろう！

タカシとレイチェルの会話を聞いて、質問に対する答えとして最も適切なものを A～C の中から1つ選びましょう。 03

Question 1　Is this the woman's first visit to Thailand?

A. Yes, it is.
B. No, it isn't. It's her second visit.
C. No, it isn't. It's her third visit.

Question 2　What is Takashi going to do in Thailand?

A. Visit some temples
B. Make presentations
C. Meet his business partners

Question 3　What is the woman's job?

A. A fashion designer
B. A fashion model
C. A website designer

LET'S CHECK & READ ALOUD! 音読してみよう！

1. スクリプトを見ながら会話をもう1度聞き、下線部に当てはまる表現を書き入れましょう。（下線部には単語が2つ入ります）
2. 内容を確認して、全文を音読してみましょう。
3. Takashi と Rachel の役割をパートナーと一緒に演じてみましょう。

Takashi: Excuse me. Is ①_____ taken?

Rachel: No, go ahead.

Takashi: Thank you. Are you flying to Bangkok today?

Rachel: Yeah. It's my ②_____ in Thailand, so I'm excited. How about you?

Takashi: Same here.

Rachel: Is your trip for business ③_____?

Takashi: Business, ④_____. I'm in charge of a new project, and I'm meeting our business partners. Are you ⑤_____ too?

Rachel: No, I'm a website designer, so I usually work at home.

Takashi: Website design? ⑥_____.

Rachel: Hmmm, I don't know. But I work ⑦_____, so I need a break. Well, I have to go now. It was nice talking to you.

Takashi: Nice talking to you too. Have a ⑧_____! Bye.

聞き取りのヒント

first time は「ファースト・タイム」ではなく「ファースタイム」のように聞こえます。このように同じ子音が連続する場合、同じ音が繰り返されるのではなく、前の子音が発音されず、その音が聞こえなくなります。例えば、this seat という語のつながりでは [s] の音が連続していますが、この音が2回聞こえるのではなく、[s] の音が1度やや長めに発音されるだけなのです。

GRAMMAR 文法に強くなろう！

A. 例にならい、カッコ内に適切な be 動詞を書き入れましょう。

   例 Mr. Smith (*is*) in a meeting now.

   1. The concert last night (　　　) wonderful.
   2. Something (　　　) wrong with this printer. Can you check it?
   3. Hurry up! You (　　　) already late.
   4. Bob and I (　　　) in the same office, but now he's in the New York office.

B. 例にならい、AとBの対話が成り立つように枠の中から適切な疑問詞を選んで文を完成させましょう。

   例 A: *What is* your favorite sport?
       B: Basketball.

   1. A: Excuse me. _____ the restroom?
      B: At the end of the hall.
   2. A: _____ the woman in this picture?
      B: That's my boss, Ms. Brown.
   3. A: _____ your parents?
      B: They're fine. Thank you for asking.
   4. A: _____ it from here to the station?
      B: About one kilometer, I think.

what ✓	which
when	how
who	how much
where	how far
why	

C. 日本語の意味に合うようにカッコ内の語句を並び替え、英文を完成させましょう。ただし、文の始めにくる単語も小文字にしてあります。

   1. 本社はどこにあるのですか？
      (is / head office / your company / of / the / where)?
      _____

   2. 会社の規模はどのくらいなのですか？
      (large / is / company / how / your)?
      _____

   3. 音声の調子が悪いです。
      (there / with / a / is / problem / the audio).
      _____

   4. 出張の後でとても疲れていました。
      I (tired / after / was / the / business trip / very).
      _____

LET'S READ!

次のパッセージを読んで1～3の質問に答えましょう。

Doing Business in Thailand

Meeting foreign business partners can be an enjoyable experience. But you may have problems if you don't understand cultural differences. If you visit Thailand, learning about Thai etiquette and manners will help you.

- When Thai people say hello, they often press their hands together. This is called "wai" and is their common greeting. Learn the rules for this greeting before using it!
- Be careful with body language. The head is very important to Thai people. You should never touch someone's head, or pass anything over someone's head. But feet are considered unclean, so try not to point your feet at anyone.

1. If you don't learn about etiquette and manners you may have _____.
    A. enjoyment
    B. a greeting
    C. trouble

2. What is a "wai"?
    A. It's a gesture to say hello.
    B. It's a traditional Thai dish.
    C. It's a way of doing business.

3. Which statement is correct?
    A. In Thailand, you should never point your head at someone.
    B. Touching someone's head is bad manners in Thailand.
    C. When you greet people, you have to say "wai."

NOTES

experience: 経験　　cultural: 文化の　　difference: 相違　　point: ～を向ける
statement: 文　　correct: 正しい

CHALLENGE YOURSELF!

リスニングテストで自分の力を試してみましょう。

Part I • Photographs

A~Cの英文を聞いて写真の描写として最も適切なものを選びましょう。

1.

   A   B   C

2.

   A   B   C

Part II • Question-Response

最初に聞こえてくる英文に対する応答として最も適切なものをA~Cの中から選びましょう。

3. A   B   C
4. A   B   C

Part III • Short Conversations

会話を聞き、下の英文が会話の内容とあっていればT（True）、間違っていればF（False）を○で囲みましょう。

5. Ms. Miller is on lunch break now.　　　　　　　　　　T　F
6. The woman isn't happy with the man's help.　　　　　T　F

LET'S READ ALOUD & WRITE! 音読筆写で覚えよう！

授業のまとめとして、今日学習した対話文を3回書き写してしっかり覚えましょう。1度英文を声に出して読んでから書き写すと頭に残りやすくなります。

今日の一言

Knowledge is power.（知識は力なり）

UNIT 02 How do you like Bangkok?

文法 現在形・過去形 2

出張先のバンコクに到着したタカシのもとに、取引先のアンジェラが訪ねてきます。会話では、挨拶したり、詳細を尋ねたりする表現を学びます。また、文法では**一般動詞（現在形・過去形）**に焦点を当てて学習します。

WARM-UP 授業前に確認しておこう！

Vocabulary Preview

1〜10の語句の意味として適切なものを a〜j の中から選びましょう。 CD 07

1. late _____   a. 飛行機の旅、空の旅
2. traffic _____   b. エアコン
3. tired _____   c. 伝統的な
4. actually _____   d. ワクワクさせる、刺激的な
5. heavy _____   e. 腹ペコで
6. exciting _____   f. （量・程度など）猛烈な、激しい
7. traditional _____   g. 疲れた
8. starving _____   h. 交通（量）
9. flight _____   i. 遅刻して
10. air-conditioner _____ j. 実際は、実は

ビートに乗って1〜10の語句を発音してみましょう。

Grammar Point 現在形・過去形 2

What do you <u>do</u>? （お仕事は何をされているのですか？）
I <u>work</u> for a software company. （ソフトウェアの会社に勤めています）

be 動詞以外の動詞を**一般動詞**と呼びますが、主語が3人称・単数・現在形の場合には動詞の語尾に s や es がつきますので注意が必要です。下の表の空欄に適切な動詞の形を書き入れて確認しましょう。

> a, i, u, e, o のことを**母音字**、それ以外を**子音字**と言います。

多くの動詞		語尾に s をつける	read → reads	live → lives make →
-s, -sh, -ch, -x, 〈子音字＋o〉で終わる動詞		語尾に es をつける	teach → teaches do → does	finish → go →
y で終わる動詞	母音字＋y の場合	語尾に s をつける	pay → pays	say →
	子音字＋y の場合	y を i に変えて es をつける	try → tries	study →
例外的な動詞		不規則な変化をする	have → has	

14

一般動詞の文を否定文にするときは、動詞のすぐ前に don't（= do not）をつけます。また疑問文にするには文の始めに do を持ってきます。主語が3人称・単数・現在の場合は doesn't や does を使い、動詞は s や es を外してもとの形（＝原形）に戻します。下の例文の日本語訳を完成させながら確認しましょう。

The air-conditioner in my room **doesn't** work. （＿＿＿＿＿＿＿＿＿＿＿＿＿＿＿＿）

Do you often go on business trips? （＿＿＿＿＿＿＿＿＿＿＿＿＿＿＿＿）

過去形にする場合は語尾に ed をつけますが、不規則に変化するものも多いので注意が必要です。巻末資料を参考にしながら下の表の空欄に適切な動詞の形を書き入れ確認しましょう。

ほとんどの動詞		語尾に ed をつける	help → helped	listen → listened
-e で終わる動詞		語尾に d をつける	like → liked	use →
y で終わる動詞	母音字＋y の場合	語尾に ed をつける	enjoy → enjoyed	play →
	子音字＋y の場合	y を i に変えて ed をつける	study → studied	carry →
母音字1つ＋子音字1つで終わる動詞		語尾の子音を重ねて ed をつける	plan → planned	stop →
例外的な動詞		不規則な変化をする	do → did go → went	have → write →

一般動詞を使った過去形の文を否定文にするときは、動詞のすぐ前に didn't（= did not）をつけます。また疑問文にするには文の始めに did を持ってきます。いずれの場合も動詞は原形に戻します。下の例文の日本語訳を完成させながら確認しましょう。

Did you have a good vacation? （＿＿＿＿＿＿＿＿＿＿＿＿＿＿＿＿）

We **didn't** get a bonus last year. （＿＿＿＿＿＿＿＿＿＿＿＿＿＿＿＿）

LET'S LISTEN! 会話の大意を聞き取ろう！

タカシとアンジェラの会話を聞いて、質問に対する答えとして最も適切なものを A〜C の中から1つ選びましょう。 08

Question 1 What did Takashi do after his flight?

A. He worked in his room.
B. He slept in his room.
C. He went shopping.

Question 2 What does Takashi think of Bangkok?

A. The traffic is heavy.
B. The city is much better than before.
C. The city is very exciting.

Question 3 What are they probably going to do next?

A. Eat dinner at the restaurant
B. Go to the woman's office
C. Cook some Thai dishes

LET'S CHECK & READ ALOUD! 音読してみよう！

1. スクリプトを見ながら会話をもう1度聞き、下線部に当てはまる表現を書き入れましょう。（下線部には単語が2つ入ります） 08
2. 内容を確認して、全文を音読してみましょう。
3. Takashi と Angela の役割をパートナーと一緒に演じてみましょう。

Angela: Hi, Takashi. ①_____ see you. How are you?

Takashi: Fine. It's good to be here.

Angela: Sorry I'm late. The traffic was ②_____.

Takashi: Well, that's OK. Actually, I was tired after my flight, so I ③_____ a few hours.

Angela: Uh-huh. Did you have a ④_____?

Takashi: Yes, I did. I feel much better now.

Angela: That's good to hear. How do you like Bangkok?

Takashi: I ⑤_____. It's very exciting, but it's so hot! I'm glad that the air-conditioner in my room ⑥_____.

Angela: OK. So let's go to the restaurant and eat. You can enjoy ⑦_____ Thai food.

Takashi: Great. ⑧_____.

聞き取りのヒント

実際の会話では、1語ずつ区切って発音されることはなく、単語と単語がつながって聞こえることがあります。これを「音の連結」と言い、例えば like it は「ライキッ(ト)」のように聞こえます。「連結」は、「子音で終わる単語」の後に「母音で始まる単語」が続いた場合によく起こります。

GRAMMAR 文法に強くなろう！

A. 例にならい枠の中から適切な単語を選び、現在形もしくは過去形の適切な形にして次の1〜4の文を完成させましょう。

例　Kate (made) a presentation yesterday.

1. My job is interesting. I (　　　　) a lot of people.
2. The accident (　　　　) last night.
3. Mr. Collins is a translator and (　　　　) five languages.
4. Maria came into the room and (　　　　) off her coat.

meet	happen
speak	take
make ✓	

B. 例にならい、AとBの対話が成り立つように枠の中から適切な動詞を選んで文を完成させましょう。主語はカッコ内の単語を使いましょう。

例　A: Did you go there on foot? How long _did it take_ ? (it)
　　B: Two hours.

1. A: What _____ ? (you)
   B: I'm a teacher.
2. A: How _____ to work? (you)
   B: Usually by train. It takes about one hour.
3. A: I missed the last train, so I came home by taxi.
   B: How much _____? (it)
   A: Fifty dollars.
4. A: How _____ your new job? (you)
   B: I love it. It's great.

take ✓	cost
do	get
like	

C. 日本語の意味に合うようにカッコ内の語句を並び替え、英文を完成させましょう。ただし、文の始めにくる単語も小文字にしてあります。

1. 上司は会議であまりしゃべりませんでした。
   (boss / not / much / my / talk / did) at the meeting.
   _____

2. 会社には何時に着きますか？
   (time / you / what / work / get to / do) ?
   _____

3. 我が社の新商品はあまり売れませんでした。
   (our / product / didn't / new / sell / very well) .
   _____

4. 出張で海外に行くことがありますか？
   (abroad / do / go / on / business / you) trips?
   _____

LET'S READ!

アンジェラがタカシに送った電子メールを読んで1～3の質問に答えましょう。

To: Takashi Kudo
From: Angela Smith
Subject: Change of plan

Dear Takashi,
So sorry to trouble you, but I'm afraid my boss can't meet you today. Instead, Mr. Kantama will pick you up at the hotel and take you to our factory. The traffic may make him a little late, so please wait in your room. He'll call you when he arrives.
Mr. Kantama is in charge of design, so he can give you a tour of the factory and explain the details. His English isn't so good, so please speak slowly for him! I'll join you after the tour.

All the best
Angela

---

1. Which statement is correct?
    A. Takashi should meet Angela's boss at the factory.
    B. Takashi should meet Mr. Kantama in the lobby.
    C. Takashi should wait for a call from Mr. Kantama.

2. What does Angela suggest to Takashi?
    A. He should speak slowly for Mr. Kantama.
    B. He should cancel the tour of the factory.
    C. He should explain the details for her.

3. When will Angela meet Takashi?
    A. When she arrives at the hotel
    B. During the factory tour
    C. After the factory tour

NOTES

pick up: 車で迎えに行く　　factory: 工場　　suggest: 提案する

CHALLENGE YOURSELF!

リスニングテストで自分の力を試してみましょう。

Part I • Photographs

A〜Cの英文を聞いて写真の描写として最も適切なものを選びましょう。

1.　　A　　B　　C

2.　　A　　B　　C

Part II • Question-Response

最初に聞こえてくる英文に対する応答として最も適切なものをA〜Cの中から選びましょう。

3.　A　　B　　C

4.　A　　B　　C

Part III • Short Conversations

会話を聞き、下の英文が会話の内容とあっていればT（True）、間違っていればF（False）を○で囲みましょう。

5. The man is very happy with his new job.　　　　　　T　　F
6. The man took the train for his trip.　　　　　　　　T　　F

LET'S READ ALOUD & WRITE! 音読筆写で覚えよう！

授業のまとめとして、今日学習した対話文を3回書き写してしっかり覚えましょう。1度英文を声に出して読んでから書き写すと頭に残りやすくなります。

今日の一言

A good beginning makes a good ending.（初めが肝心）

UNIT 03 It's going well so far.

文法 進行形・未来形

タカシはバンコクにある取引先の社内をアンジェラに案内してもらった後、彼女と打ち合わせをします。会話では、お礼を述べたり、予定を確認したりする表現を学びます。また、文法では**進行形**と**未来形**に焦点を当てて学習します。

WARM-UP 授業前に確認しておこう！

Vocabulary Preview

1～10の語句の意味として適切なものをa～jの中から選びましょう。　CD 12

1. produce _____	a. ～を案内する
2. so far _____	b. 予定通りで
3. colleague _____	c. 同僚
4. go well _____	d. うまく行く
5. final _____	e. 広告代理店
6. show around _____	f. 最終の、確定した
7. on schedule _____	g. 今までのところ
8. What about...? _____	h. ～はどうですか？
9. behind schedule _____	i. 生産する
10. ad agency _____	j. 予定より遅れて

ビートに乗って1～10の語句を発音してみましょう。

Grammar Point　進行形・未来形

We're having a meeting now. （現在会議中です）
I'm meeting my client this afternoon. （午後お客さんに会う予定です）
I'll check my schedule and get back to you. （予定を確認してご連絡いたします）

現在形が日常的な内容を指すのに対し、今している最中の動作を表す場合には**現在進行形**を用い、《am / is / are（be動詞）＋動詞のing形》の形で表します。下の表の空欄に適切な動詞の形を書き入れてing形の作り方を確認しましょう。

ほとんどの動詞	語尾にingをつける	work → working	send → sending
子音＋eで終わる動詞	語尾のeを取ってingをつける	make → making	take →
-ie [ai] で終わる動詞	語尾のieをyに変えてingをつける	die → dying	lie →
母音＋子音で終わる動詞	語尾の子音字を重ねてingをつける	get → getting	begin →

現在進行形は、「〜している」のように、今実際にしていることだけではなく、決まった予定や何度も繰り返されている動作を表すこともあります。また、be 動詞の過去形を使って**過去進行形**にすると「〜していた」という意味を表します。下の例文の日本語訳を完成させながら使い方を確認しましょう。

You're always working. Take a few days off. (　　　　　　　　　　　　　　)

I was having lunch at that time. (　　　　　　　　　　　　　　)

次に、これから先のことを話す場合には、《be going to ＋動詞の原形》や《will ＋動詞の原形》、現在進行形など、いくつか方法があります。下の表で確認しましょう。

> will はその場でそうすると決めたのに対し、be going to はすでにその予定でいたことを表します。

will	意志（〜するつもりだ）	I'll ask the boss.
	予測（〜だろう）	Hurry up, or we'll miss the last train.
be going to	予測（〜だろう）	Look at the clouds. It's going to rain.
	計画や意志（〜するつもりだ）	I'm going to study abroad next year.
現在進行形	すでに決まっている予定や計画	What are you doing after work today?

> will not = won't

will を使った文を否定文にするには will の後に not をつけ、疑問文にするには will を主語の前に持ってきます。下の例文の日本語訳を完成させながら使い方を確認しましょう。

I'm very sorry. This won't happen again.
(　　　　　　　　　　　　　　　　　　　　　　　　)

When will the report be ready?
(　　　　　　　　　　　　　　　　　　　　　　　　)

What are you going to do this weekend?
(　　　　　　　　　　　　　　　　　　　　　　　　)

LET'S LISTEN! 会話の大意を聞き取ろう！

タカシとアンジェラの会話を聞いて、質問に対する答えとして最も適切なものをA〜Cの中から1つ選びましょう。 13

Question 1 How is the design for the new model going?

A. It's on schedule.
B. It's behind schedule.
C. It's already finished.

Question 2 When will the final design be ready?

A. Next week
B. At the end of this month
C. Next month

Question 3 When will they start producing the new model?

A. Next week
B. At the end of this month
C. Next month

LET'S CHECK & READ ALOUD! 音読してみよう!

1. スクリプトを見ながら会話をもう1度聞き、下線部に当てはまる表現を書き入れましょう。(下線部には単語が2つ入ります)
2. 内容を確認して、全文を音読してみましょう。
3. Takashi と Angela の役割をパートナーと一緒に演じてみましょう。

Takashi: Thank you for showing me around. I ①_____ with your colleagues.

Angela: ②_____.

Takashi: Well, how is the design for the new model going?

Angela: ③_____ well so far. The final design will be ready by the end of this month. We're ④_____.

Takashi: Sounds great. Then we can start production next month, right?

Angela: Yes, that's right.

Takashi: What about marketing?

Angela: ⑤_____ to some ad agencies now, and ⑥_____ to choose one next month.

Takashi: OK. I hope ⑦_____ get behind schedule.

Angela: Don't worry. ⑧_____ fine.

聞き取りのヒント

クッキングやウォーキングなど、カタカナ英語の影響もあって、talking など動詞の ing 形を「トーキング」のように「〜イング」と発音する人がいますが、ing の [ŋ] における [ŋ] は「ンヶ」という感じの鼻にかけた音で、「ヶ」の音は鼻から出ていくため、はっきりとは聞こえない音です。「イング」ではなく、「インヶ」という感じです。発音する際にもぜひ気をつけたいものです。

GRAMMAR 文法に強くなろう！

A. 例にならい枠の中から適切な単語を選び、必要な場合は適切な形にして次の1～4の文を完成させましょう。3は主語として you を使いましょう。

例　It (is raining) now. Take an umbrella.

1. We (　　　　) lunch now. Can I call you later?
2. Turn off the television. I (　　　　) now.
3. "What (　　　　) now?" "I'm writing an e-mail to my boss."
4. Sorry, I can't talk now. I (　　　　) my client.

```
do      meet
have    work
rain ✓
```

B. 例にならいカッコ内から正しい語句を選び○で囲みましょう。

例　Look at the clouds. It (will / (is going to)) rain.

1. I can't go out with you tonight. Sorry. (I'll work / I'm working) overtime.
2. "Is Tom coming to the party?" "Wait, (I'll / I'm going to) ask him."
3. I'm sorry. I (won't / will) make the same mistake again.
4. "What (do you do / are you doing) tonight?" "Nothing. I have no plans."

C. 日本語の意味に合うようにカッコ内の語句を並び替え、英文を完成させましょう。ただし、文の始めにくる単語も小文字にしてあります。

1. すべて順調ですか？

　(everything / is / well / you / with / going) ?

　_____

2. 販売報告書はいつ用意できるのですか？

　(when / the / ready / be / sales report / will) ?

　_____

3. 私は明日の会議でプレゼンをする予定です。

　(going / make / I'm / a presentation / at / to) the meeting tomorrow.

　_____

4. 出張の準備をしているのかい？

　(preparing / your / are / business trip / for / you) ?

　_____

LET'S READ!

次のパッセージを読んで1～3の質問に答えましょう。

Go with the Flow!

Takashi is nervous about their business partner's ability to stay on schedule and meet the deadline. In Japan, being on time is very important in business. But people from other cultures such as the Middle East, South America, or Africa may have a very different approach. For them, being on time may not be so important.

In such situations, just "Go with the flow" and enjoy a different way of doing things. Actually, Takashi doesn't need to worry about the deadline. If they don't have traffic jams, Thai people usually stay on schedule, just like the Japanese!

1. Which statement is correct?
    A. Takashi believes that their partner's work will be on time.
    B. Takashi is worried that their partner's work will be late.
    C. Takashi will meet his deadline.

2. People's attitude towards time is influenced by _____.
    A. culture
    B. deadlines
    C. flow

3. The Thai attitude towards time is similar to that of _____.
    A. people in the Middle East
    B. people in South America
    C. the Japanese

NOTES

nervous: 心配して　　deadline: 締め切り　　jam: 渋滞　　attitude: 態度、考え方

CHALLENGE YOURSELF!

リスニングテストで自分の力を試してみましょう。

Part I • Photographs

A～Cの英文を聞いて写真の描写として最も適切なものを選びましょう。

1.　　A　　B　　C

2.　　A　　B　　C

Part II • Question-Response

最初に聞こえてくる英文に対する応答として最も適切なものをA～Cの中から選びましょう。

3.　A　　B　　C

4.　A　　B　　C

Part III • Short Conversations

会話を聞き、下の英文が会話の内容とあっていればT（True）、間違っていればF（False）を○で囲みましょう。

5. The woman has a problem, so she wants to talk to the man.　　T　　F

6. The man wants to contact Sally.　　T　　F

LET'S READ ALOUD & WRITE! 音読筆写で覚えよう！

授業のまとめとして、今日学習した対話文を3回書き写してしっかり覚えましょう。1度英文を声に出して読んでから書き写すと頭に残りやすくなります。

今日の一言

Perseverance will win in the end.
（最後には忍耐が勝つ／石の上にも3年）

UNIT 04 Have they decided on the design yet?

文法　現在完了形

バンコクへの出張から帰ってきたタカシに上司のジュリアが声をかけ出張のことについていろいろと質問をします。会話では、経験を述べたり、指示したりする表現を学びます。また、文法では**現在完了形**に焦点を当てて学習します。

WARM-UP　授業前に確認しておこう！

Vocabulary Preview

1〜10の語句の意味として適切なものをa〜jの中から選びましょう。　CD 17

1. helpful	_____	a.	〜に連絡を取る
2. detail	_____	b.	（〜を）見つけ出す
3. decide	_____	c.	決める
4. yet	_____	d.	必ず〜するように手配する
5. glad	_____	e.	（否定文で）まだ〜ない、（疑問文で）もう
6. find out	_____	f.	詳細
7. contact	_____	g.	うれしく思って
8. make sure	_____	h.	助けになる
9. left	_____	i.	間に合うように、時間内に
10. in time	_____	j.	残された

ビートに乗って1〜10の語句を発音してみましょう。

Grammar Point　現在完了形

> 否定文にするには have/has の後に not をつけます。

Mr. Kimura <u>has fixed</u> this computer, so you can use it now.
（木村さんがこのパソコンを直してくれたので、もう使えますよ）

My train <u>hasn't arrived</u> yet.
（私の乗る電車はまだ到着していません）

> 疑問文にするには have/has を主語の前に持ってきます。

<u>Have</u> you <u>started</u> your new job yet?
（新しい仕事はもう始めたのですか？）

　過去にしたことや過去に起こったことを現在と結びつけて話す場合には**現在完了形**を用い、《have / has ＋過去分詞》という形で表します。主語が he など3人称単数の場合は have ではなく has を使います。

　過去分詞は、talk → talked（過去形）→ talked（過去分詞）のように、多くの場合動詞の過去形と同じ形ですが、give → gave（過去形）→ given（過去分詞）のように不規則に変化するものも多くあります。次の表を完成させると共に、巻末の不規則動詞変化表でも確認しておきましょう。

不規則動詞の変化パターン		原形	過去形	過去分詞形
A-A-A	原形、過去形、過去分詞がすべて同じ	cost cut	cost cut	cost cut
A-B-A	原形と過去分詞が同じ	become come run	became	become
A-B-B	過去形と過去分詞が同じ	say tell think	said	said
A-B-C	原形、過去形、過去分詞がすべて異なる	eat go know	ate	eaten

　また、現在完了形の表す意味にはいくつか種類があります。次の表の例文の日本語訳を完成させながらそれぞれの意味を確認しましょう。

完了	〜したところだ	"Are you hungry?" "No. We've just eaten lunch." (　　　　　　　　　　　　　　　　　　　　　　　　　　　)
	〜してしまった	I've lost my passport. What should I do? (　　　　　　　　　　　　　　　　　　　　　　　　　　　)
経験	〜したことがある	"Has Rachel ever been to Bangkok?" "Yes, once." (　　　　　　　　　　　　　　　　　　　　　　　　　　　)
継続	ずっと〜している	My parents have been married for thirty years. (　両親は　　　　　　　　　　　　　　　　　　　　　　　)

　現在完了形は、あくまで現在の状況を述べる言い方なので、yesterday 等、明確に過去の時点を表す表現とは一緒に使うことができません。

LET'S LISTEN!　会話の大意を聞き取ろう！

タカシとジュリアの会話を聞いて、質問に対する答えとして最も適切なものを A 〜 C の中から 1 つ選びましょう。 18

Question 1　What did Takashi say about the food in Bangkok?

　A. It was very good.

　B. It was too spicy.

　C. It was OK.

Question 2　Has Julia been to Bangkok?

　A. Yes, many times.

　B. Yes, once.

　C. No, she hasn't.

Question 3　What is Takashi probably going to do next?

　A. Call Angela

　B. Decide on the design

　C. Go to Angela's office

LET'S CHECK & READ ALOUD! 音読してみよう！

1. スクリプトを見ながら会話をもう1度聞き、下線部に当てはまる表現を書き入れましょう。（下線部には単語が2つ入ります） 18
2. 内容を確認して、全文を音読してみましょう。
3. Takashi と Julia の役割をパートナーと一緒に演じてみましょう。

Julia: Hello, Takashi. Did you have a ①_____ to Bangkok?

Takashi: Yes, I did. Angela was very helpful, and I had a good time there.

Julia: ②_____ hear that. I've never ③_____. How was the food?

Takashi: It was wonderful.

Julia: Great. Well, I ④_____ check some details about the new model. Have they ⑤_____ the design yet?

Takashi: No, not yet. The final design will be ready by the end of this month.

Julia: We have only two ⑥_____. Please make sure you get it in time.

Takashi: I'll call her this afternoon and find out.

Julia: Fine. Can you ⑦_____ to me about that?

Takashi: Sure. I'll ⑧_____ office and get back to you soon.

聞き取りのヒント

同じ子音が続く場合だけでなく、[d]と[t]、[g]と[k]、[p]と[b]など、発音の仕方の似た子音が続く場合も、前の子音ははっきり発音されず、聞こえにくくなります。例えば、good time は「グッタイム」、next door は「ネクスドア」のように聞こえます。聞き取りのヒントは発音する際のヒントにもなりますから、good time が「グッドタイム」とならないように発音しましょう。

GRAMMAR 文法に強くなろう！

A. 例にならい枠の中から適切な単語を選び、必要な場合は適切な形にして次の1～4の文を完成させましょう。

　例　The weather (was) very good yesterday.

```
get     arrive
live    eat
be ✓
```

1. "How about lunch together?" "Sorry. I've just (　　　　)."
2. Mark (　　　　) married three years ago.
3. "Is Carol here?" "Yes, she's just (　　　　)."
4. I live in Tokyo now, but I (　　　　) in Nagoya for many years.

B. 例にならいカッコ内から正しい語句を選び○で囲みましょう。

　例　Rachel has been in Japan ((since) / for) Monday.

1. We (finished / have finished) this project three months ago.
2. Mark and I are friends. (I know / I've known) him for five years.
3. (Have you seen / Did you see) Kate yesterday?
4. Laura (works / has worked) in a bookstore now. She likes her job a lot.

C. 日本語の意味に合うようにカッコ内の語句を並び替え、英文を完成させましょう。ただし、文の始めにくる単語も小文字にしてあります。

1. 知り合ってどれくらいになるのですか？

   (have / known / each / long / you / how) other?

   _____

2. 私は英語でプレゼンをしたことがありません。

   (never / a presentation / I've / English / in / made).

   _____

3. 私たちは月曜日からバンコクに来ています。

   We (in / been / Monday / since / Bangkok / have).

   _____

4. ここで働いて3年になります。

   (been / for / working / three / here / I've) years.

   _____

LET'S READ!

タカシが友人のテリーに書いた下のハガキを読んで1〜3の質問に答えましょう。

Hi Terry

As promised, a postcard from Bangkok! My business trip has gone smoothly, and I even had a little time for sightseeing. Thanks again for your advice. It was really helpful. The river cruise on the Chao Phraya was unbelievable, and the hotel was really good. People here are so friendly, and of course, the food is fantastic! I hope to come here again sometime. I haven't had time to contact your friend Sonthida yet, but I'll make sure to do it before my flight leaves on Thursday. Anyway, no space left! Thanks again.
Take care.

Takashi

1. Which statement is correct?
    A. Takashi wishes he had more time for business.
    B. Takashi's business trip was full of problems.
    C. Takashi's business trip was successful.

2. In his postcard, Takashi wrote "no space left!" This means that _____.
    A. Takashi has no more time
    B. Takashi's hotel room is very small, and he can't write
    C. the postcard is too small for Takashi's message

3. Which statement is correct?
    A. Takashi met Sonthida and enjoyed dinner with her.
    B. Takashi hopes to meet Sonthida before returning home.
    C. Takashi won't have time to meet Sonthida this time.

NOTES

as promised: 約束したように   **sightseeing:** 観光
Chao Phraya: チャオプラヤー川   **Sonthida:** ソンティーダ

CHALLENGE YOURSELF!

リスニングテストで自分の力を試してみましょう。

Part I • Photographs

A～Cの英文を聞いて写真の描写として最も適切なものを選びましょう。

1.

   A   B   C

2.

   A   B   C

Part II • Question-Response

最初に聞こえてくる英文に対する応答として最も適切なものをA～Cの中から選びましょう。

3.   A   B   C
4.   A   B   C

Part III • Short Conversations

会話を聞き、下の英文が会話の内容とあっていればT（True）、間違っていればF（False）を○で囲みましょう。

5. The man wants to eat at the Mexican restaurant.   T   F
6. The man has lost his computer.   T   F

LET'S READ ALOUD & WRITE! 音読筆写で覚えよう！

授業のまとめとして、今日学習した対話文を3回書き写してしっかり覚えましょう。1度英文を声に出して読んでから書き写すと頭に残りやすくなります。

今日の一言

Anyone who has never made a mistake has never tried anything new.
（失敗をしたことがない人は何も新しいことに挑戦したことがない人だ）
Albert Einstein（1879-1955）

UNIT 05 Could you take a look at them?

文法 助動詞

プレゼンを控えたタカシは上司のジュリアを訪ね、プレゼンで使うスライドのことについて相談をします。会話では、依頼をしたり、助言をしたりする表現を学びます。また、文法では**助動詞**に焦点を当てて学習します。

WARM-UP 授業前に確認しておこう！

Vocabulary Preview

1〜10の語句の意味として適切なものを a〜j の中から選びましょう。

🎧 22

1. illustration	_____	a. すぐに
2. information	_____	b. 〜よりはむしろ
3. revise	_____	c. 概念、考え
4. concept	_____	d. 見る
5. sentence	_____	e. 〜を修正する
6. definitely	_____	f. 図、絵
7. right away	_____	g.〔意味・考えなどを〕理解させる
8. get across	_____	h. 文
9. take a look	_____	i. その通り、もちろん
10. rather than	_____	j. 情報

ビートに乗って 1〜10 の語句を発音してみましょう。

Grammar Point 助動詞

You **must** be tired.　　　　　（きっとお疲れでしょう）
Could you do me a favor?　（お願いがあるのですが）

助動詞は**動詞の前につけて動詞に意味を追加するもの**です。助動詞の場合、一般動詞と違って主語が3人称単数であっても語尾に -s や -es がつくことはありません。

must の否定形 must not は「〜してはいけない」という意味になり、「〜する必要はない」と言いたい場合は don't have to... を使います。

主な助動詞とその用法は下の表の通りです。

> 疑問文にするときは助動詞を文の始めに置きます。

can	〜できる（be able to） 〜してもよい	1. How **can** I help you? 2. Hello. **Can** I speak to John, please?
must	〜しなければならない（have to） 〜に違いない	3. You **must** attend the meeting tomorrow. 4. You **must** be joking.
may	〜してもよい 〜かもしれない	5. **May** I use this computer for a minute? 6. I **may** be late this evening.

might	～かもしれない	7. Henry <u>might</u> be able to help you.
should	～すべきである	8. You <u>shouldn't</u> be late.
used to	以前は～だった	9. Bob <u>used to</u> work in a factory.

> 否定文にするときは助動詞のすぐ後に not をつけます。

また、would や could はそれぞれ助動詞 will と can の過去形ですが、実際のコミュニケーションにおいては必ずしも過去の意味で使うのではなく、丁寧な言い方をする場合によく用いられます。下の表に挙げるものは実際に仕事をする場面でよく使われるものばかりです。

would like	～が欲しい	want や want to よりも丁寧で控えめな感じがします。
would like to	～したい	
Would you...?	～して頂けないでしょうか	Will you...? や Can you...? よりも丁寧で控えめな感じがします。
Could you...?		

下の例文の日本語訳を完成させながら使い方を確認しましょう。

I'm sorry, I <u>can't</u> hear you. <u>Can</u> you speak louder, please?

(　　　　　　　　　　　　　　　　　　　　　　　　　　)

I didn't catch that. <u>Could</u> you say that again?

(　　　　　　　　　　　　　　　　　　　　　　　　　　)

<u>Would</u> you <u>like to</u> leave a message?

(　　　　　　　　　　　　　　　　　　　　　　　　　　)

LET'S LISTEN! 会話の大意を聞き取ろう！

タカシとジュリアの会話を聞いて、質問に対する答えとして最も適切なものを A～C の中から１つ選びましょう。 23

Question 1　What does Takashi ask Julia to do?

A. Make slides for his presentation
B. Check the slides
C. Add some slides

Question 2　What is Julia's advice?

A. Use larger fonts
B. Use more animations
C. Use more color

Question 3　What is Takashi probably going to do next?

A. Ask someone for help
B. Make a presentation
C. Revise the slides

LET'S CHECK & READ ALOUD! 音読してみよう！

 23

1. スクリプトを見ながら会話をもう1度聞き、下線部に当てはまる表現を書き入れましょう。（下線部には単語が2つ入ります）
2. 内容を確認して、全文を音読してみましょう。
3. Takashi と Julia の役割をパートナーと一緒に演じてみましょう。

Takashi: Excuse me, but can I talk to you for a minute?

Julia: Sure. ①_____ ?

Takashi: I'm preparing for my presentation and I'm not sure if my slides are OK. Could you take a look at them?

Julia: No problem. Well, ②_____. Your slides look fine. But you put too much information into one slide.

Takashi: Do you really think so? I thought the sentences were ③_____.

Julia: No, they're still too long. Use keywords ④_____ sentences. Also, you ⑤_____ to use larger fonts.

Takashi: All right. Any other comments? ⑥_____ use more illustrations?

Julia: Definitely. They're useful to ⑦_____ your key concepts.

Takashi: Right. ⑧_____ the slides right away.

聞き取りのヒント

単語の最後にくる [l] は、つづり字からつい「ル」に近い音を予想しますが、実際には「ゥ」のように聞こえます。例えば、all [ɔ́ːl] は「オール」ではなく、むしろ「オーゥ」のように聞こえます。well [wél] は「ウェル」ではなく「ウェゥ」のような感じです。I'll もつい「アイル」と発音しがちですが、「アィゥ」が実際の発音に近いものです。

GRAMMAR 文法に強くなろう！

A. 例にならい枠の中から適切な語句を選んで次の1〜4の文を完成させましょう。

例　I (*would like*) a flight to New York, please.

1. Take an umbrella with you. It (　　　) rain.
2. Tom is always telling lies. You (　　　) believe him.
3. There (　　　) be a supermarket here.
4. You don't (　　　) decide now. Take your time.

> shouldn't
> used to
> have to
> might
> would like ✓

B. 例にならいカッコ内から正しい語句を選び○で囲みましょう。

例　I don't believe that story. It (can /(can't)) be true.

1. The sign "Keep out" means that you (don't have to / must not) enter.
2. (Could I / Could you) have your name, please?
3. (I'd like / I'd like to) a table for three.
4. "What (do you like / would you like) to drink?" "A coffee, please."

C. 日本語の意味に合うようにカッコ内の語句を並び替え、英文を完成させましょう。ただし、文の始めにくる単語も小文字にしてあります。

1. すみません。（電話）番号を間違えたようです。
   I'm sorry. (must / the / I / have / number / wrong).
   _____

2. もう少しゆっくり話して頂けませんか？
   (speak / you / slowly / more / could) ?
   _____

3. このソフトウェアを試してみるとよいかもね。
   (you / this software / want / try / to / might).
   _____

4. お座りになりませんか？
   (like / you / sit / to / down / would) ?
   _____

LET'S READ!

次のパッセージを読んで1〜3の質問に答えましょう。

Death by PowerPoint

Using PowerPoint may help your presentation, but may also cause problems, such as "Death by PowerPoint." This happens when a presentation becomes so boring that the listeners feel like they are dying!

If you don't want to have this problem, just follow these rules:

- When possible, use pictures and graphs.
- Choose colors carefully. (Red text on a green background?! Please! Stop!)
  But perhaps the most important is...
- Don't use more than 20 words per slide. Reading aloud a slide full of words will kill your listener's interest. And it's really bad for business.

1. Death by PowerPoint happens when _____.
    A. the presentation is not interesting
    B. the speaker is very old
    C. there are too many images

2. According to the passage, red text on a green background is _____.
    A. a great idea
    B. often used
    C. a very bad idea

3. According to the passage, we can avoid "Death by PowerPoint" if we _____.
    A. turn on the lights and serve snacks
    B. make the presentation longer
    C. use fewer words in the slides

NOTES

cause: 引き起こす　　　**per:** 〜につき　　　**aloud:** 声を出して
according to: 〜によれば

CHALLENGE YOURSELF!

リスニングテストで自分の力を試してみましょう。

Part I • Photographs

A〜Cの英文を聞いて写真の描写として最も適切なものを選びましょう。 24

1.　　A　　B　　C

2.　　A　　B　　C

Part II • Question-Response

最初に聞こえてくる英文に対する応答として最も適切なものをA〜Cの中から選びましょう。 25

3.　A　　B　　C

4.　A　　B　　C

Part III • Short Conversations

会話を聞き、下の英文が会話の内容とあっていればT（True）、間違っていればF（False）を○で囲みましょう。 26

5. The meeting will be held on Friday.　　　　　　　　　　T　　F
6. The woman wants to take a few days off.　　　　　　　T　　F

LET'S READ ALOUD & WRITE! 音読筆写で覚えよう！

授業のまとめとして、今日学習した対話文を3回書き写してしっかり覚えましょう。1度英文を声に出して読んでから書き写すと頭に残りやすくなります。

今日の一言

Peace cannot be kept by force. It can only be achieved by understanding.（平和は、力によっては維持できない。それは、理解によってのみ達成される）　Albert Einstein（1879-1955）

UNIT 06 My flight was canceled.

文法 受動態

タカシのところの取引先のジョーンズ氏から電話がかかってきます。どうやらトラブルが起きたようです。会話では、事情を説明する表現や電話での応答表現を学びます。また、文法では**受動態**に焦点を当てて学習します。

WARM-UP 授業前に確認しておこう！

Vocabulary Preview

1〜10の語句の意味として適切なものを a〜j の中から選びましょう。 CD 27

1. department _____   a. 〜だと思う、仮定する
2. expect _____   b. 嵐
3. instead _____   c. 〜を中止する、〜を取り消す
4. make it _____   d. 面会の約束
5. appointment _____   e. 〜が来ると思う、待ち受ける
6. possible _____   f. 部・課
7. due to _____   g. 〜のために
8. suppose _____   h. 可能な
9. cancel _____   i. 代わりに
10. storm _____   j. 時間に間に合う

ビートに乗って1〜10の語句を発音してみましょう。

Grammar Point 受動態

<u>The president</u>　makes　<u>the final decision</u>.（社長が最終決定をします）〔能動態〕

<u>The final decision</u>　is made　by <u>the president</u>.（最終決定は社長によってなされます）〔受動態〕

「〜は…される／されている」のように、何らかの動作を受ける意味を表す場合には、**受動態**を用い、《be動詞＋過去分詞》という形で表します。これに対して、これまで学習してきた「〜は…する」のように、何かに働きかける意味を表す文を**能動態**と言います。

能動態にするか受動態にするかは、話題になっている「もの」や「こと」によって決まります。次に挙げる例文では、話題が「インターネット」なので、「使われている」と受動態が使われるわけです。

「〜によって」はbyで表します。誰がしたのかが重要でない場合には不要。

The Internet is very important in business. It <u>is used</u> around the world.
（インターネットはビジネスにおいてとても重要です。それは世界中で使われています）

この例文は"People use it around the world."のように能動態を使うこともできますが、受動態で表現する方が自然です。

また、受動態にも能動態と同じように、過去形、進行形、完了形といった時制があります。下の例文の日本語訳を完成させながら使い方を確認しましょう。

> 進行形は《be 動詞＋being ＋過去分詞》となります。

> 過去形は《was/were ＋過去分詞》となります。

The copying machine <u>was broken</u> two days ago.
(_____)

It <u>is being repaired</u> now.
(_____)

The topic <u>will be discussed</u> at the next meeting.
(_____)

> 未来形は《will be ＋過去分詞》や《be going to be ＋過去分詞》を使います。

The final decision <u>hasn't been made</u> yet.
(_____
_____)

> 現在完了形は《have/has ＋been ＋過去分詞》となります。

LET'S LISTEN! 会話の大意を聞き取ろう！

タカシとジョーンズ氏の会話を聞いて、質問に対する答えとして最も適切なものをA〜Cの中から1つ選びましょう。 28

Question 1 What does the woman want to change?

A. The place of a meeting
B. The time of a meeting
C. The date of a meeting

Question 2 What happened to the woman's flight?

A. She canceled it.
B. It was canceled.
C. She lost her ticket and missed the flight.

Question 3 What time are they going to meet?

A. At 1:30
B. At 5:00
C. At 5:30

LET'S CHECK & READ ALOUD! 音読してみよう！

1. スクリプトを見ながら会話をもう1度聞き、下線部に当てはまる表現を書き入れましょう。（下線部には単語が2つ入ります）
2. 内容を確認して、全文を音読してみましょう。
3. Takashi と Ms. Jones の役割をパートナーと一緒に演じてみましょう。

Takashi: Sales Department. How can I help you?

Ms. Jones: Hello. ①_____ speak to Mr. Takashi Kudo?

Takashi: Speaking.

Ms. Jones: Oh, Mr. Kudo. It's Sally Jones here. I'm calling about ②_____.

Takashi: Yes, Ms. Jones, ③_____ you.

Ms. Jones: But I'm afraid my flight ④_____ due to the storm. I'll take the train instead, but I can't ⑤_____ at one thirty. Is it ⑥_____ you to change the time?

Takashi: I'm sorry to hear that. When will you be able to come here?

Ms. Jones: I suppose I can ⑦_____ by five o'clock. ⑧_____ OK with you?

Takashi: Let's see. How about five thirty?

Ms. Jones: That's fine with me. Thank you very much.

DID YOU KNOW?

電話特有の表現がありますので確認しておきましょう。「～さんをお願いします」と言いたい場合は、"May I [Could I] speak to...?" を使います。それに対して「～におつなぎします」と答えたい場合は、"One moment, please. I'll put you through." と言います。また、「自分です」と答えたい場合は、"Speaking." の他、"This is he [she]." と言うこともありますが、非常に改まった言い方です。

GRAMMAR 文法に強くなろう！

A. 例にならい枠の中から適切な単語を選び、必要な場合は適切な形にして次の1〜4の文を完成させましょう。

例　Paper (*is made*) from wood.

1. My passport (　　　　　) at the airport this morning.
2. This building (　　　　　) 50 years ago.
3. Soccer (　　　　　) in many countries.
4. We (　　　　　) to the party, but we didn't go.

```
steal    build
play     invite
make ✓
```

B. 例にならいカッコ内から正しい語句を選び○で囲みましょう。

例　English (speaks / (is spoken)) in many countries.

1. The project (discussed / was discussed) at the meeting yesterday.
2. The president (made / was made) a bad decision.
3. There was an accident, and an old man was (taking / taken) to the hospital.
4. The driver (killed / was killed) in the accident.

C. 日本語の意味に合うようにカッコ内の語句を並び替え、英文を完成させましょう。ただし、文の始めにくる単語も小文字にしてあります。

1. 私のパソコンは現在修理中です。
   (computer / being / at / my / repaired / is) the moment.
   _____

2. その結果は来週連絡される予定です。
   (be / result / given / next / will / the) week.
   _____

3. コンサートは大雨のため中止になりました。
   (concert / canceled / to / due / was / the) heavy rain.
   _____

4. プレゼンは英語でされなければなりません。
   (the / in / made / be / must / presentations) English.
   _____

LET'S READ!

下のメモを読んで1〜3の質問に答えましょう。

Subject: Rescheduled meeting

Morning everyone,

I've just had a phone call from Sally Jones, chief designer from Concept Graphics ad agency. I'm afraid her flight has been canceled and she can't get here in time for the 1:30 meeting. The meeting has been rescheduled for 5:30, so please make sure you're available. If you definitely can't come, please be sure to let me know <u>right away</u>.

I expect you've already taken a look at her report. It's very detailed and useful, but it needs to be revised. How about meeting at 1:30 to discuss it?

Takashi

---

1. Sally's flight has been canceled, so Takashi _____.

    A. changes the time of the meeting

    B. is frightened

    C. says sorry to his colleagues

2. The underlined words "right away" are closest in meaning to _____.

    A. as soon as possible

    B. later

    C. sometimes

3. Which statement is true?

    A. Takashi plans to make some changes in Sally's report.

    B. Takashi will accept Sally's report.

    C. They will discuss, then reject Sally's report.

---

underlined: 下線が引かれた　　　closest in meaning to: 〜に意味が最も近い

CHALLENGE YOURSELF!

リスニングテストで自分の力を試してみましょう。

Part I • *Photographs*

A〜Cの英文を聞いて写真の描写として最も適切なものを選びましょう。　🎧 29

1.

　　　A　　B　　C

2.

　　　A　　B　　C

Part II • *Question-Response*

最初に聞こえてくる英文に対する応答として最も適切なものをA〜Cの中から選びましょう。　🎧 30

3.　A　　B　　C

4.　A　　B　　C

Part III • *Short Conversations*

会話を聞き、下の英文が会話の内容とあっていればT（True）、間違っていればF（False）を○で囲みましょう。　🎧 31

5. The man has an appointment with Ms. Wilson.　　　T　　F
6. Kate had a traffic accident and is in hospital now.　　T　　F

LET'S READ ALOUD & WRITE!　音読筆写で覚えよう！

授業のまとめとして、今日学習した対話文を3回書き写してしっかり覚えましょう。1度英文を声に出して読んでから書き写すと頭に残りやすくなります。

　今日の一言

Rome wasn't built in a day.（ローマは1日にして成らず）

UNIT 07 What do you want me to do?

文法　不定詞

仕事中のタカシにジャネットが話しかけてきます。何か手伝ってほしいことがあるようです。会話では、意向を尋ねたり、操作方法を説明したりする表現を学びます。また、文法では**不定詞**に焦点を当てて学習します。

WARM-UP　授業前に確認しておこう！

Vocabulary Preview

1～10の語句の意味として適切なものをa～jの中から選びましょう。　CD 32

1. bother　　_____　　a. ～を挿入する
2. pie chart　_____　　b. 実際
3. enter　　　_____　　c. ～を作る
4. data　　　 _____　　d. 円グラフ
5. create　　 _____　　e. ～に面倒をかける
6. get it　　 _____　　f. 選択肢、選択できるもの
7. option　　 _____　　g. データ
8. insert　　 _____　　h. 選ぶ
9. in fact　　_____　　i.（コンピュータにデータなど）を入力する
10. select　　_____　　j. 理解する、わかる

ビートに乗って1～10の語句を発音してみましょう。

Grammar Point　to 不定詞

The purpose of this meeting is <u>to make a new sales plan</u>.
（この会議の目的は新しい販売計画を作成することです）
I'm sorry <u>to trouble you</u>, but can I talk to you for a minute?
（邪魔して申し訳ないけど、少し話をしてもいいかい？）
I have a lot of reports <u>to make</u>.（作成しないといけない報告書がたくさんある）

《to ＋動詞の原形》の形を **to 不定詞**と呼びますが、その用法は下の表のように大きく3つに分けられます。

名詞的用法	～すること	Would you like **to come** to my office?
副詞的用法	～するために（目的）	Julia went to New York **to attend** a conference.
	～して（感情の原因）	I'm very happy **to hear** that.
形容詞的用法	～すべき	I have something **to tell** you.

形容詞的用法は名詞のすぐ後ろにきてその名詞を説明します。「話すべき何かを持っている」→「話がある」

また、下の表のように、to 不定詞の前に what や how などの疑問詞がついてまとまった意味を表す他、enough... to ～や too... to ～といった慣用表現もあります。

疑問詞＋ to 不定詞	Let me show you how to use the machine. （どのように～したらよいのか、～の仕方）
動詞＋人＋ to 不定詞	I want you to help me. （～に…してほしい） Julia told me to give you this report. （～に…するように言う）
enough や too を伴う 形容詞＋ to 不定詞	You are old enough to drink. （～するには十分なくらい…だ） It's too early to give up. （～するにはあまりにも…過ぎる）

下の例文の日本語訳を完成させながら使い方を確認しましょう。

Can you tell us what to do next?

(　　)

Bill was kind enough to help me with the report.

(　　)

Julia advised me to take a day off.

(　　)

LET'S LISTEN! 会話の大意を聞き取ろう！

タカシとジャネットの会話を聞いて、質問に対する答えとして最も適切なものを A ～ C の中から１つ選びましょう。

Question 1　What does Janet want to know?

　A. How to create charts
　B. How to fix a computer
　C. How to make apple pies

Question 2　What is Takashi doing now?

　A. Writing an e-mail
　B. Having a coffee break
　C. Making a sales report

Question 3　What is the first step?

　A. Click the "Insert" menu.
　B. Select "Chart" from the list of options.
　C. Enter your data.

LET'S CHECK & READ ALOUD! 音読してみよう！

1. スクリプトを見ながら会話をもう1度聞き、下線部に当てはまる表現を書き入れましょう。（下線部には単語が2つ入ります） 🎧 33
2. 内容を確認して、全文を音読してみましょう。
3. Takashi と Janet の役割をパートナーと一緒に演じてみましょう。

Janet: I'm sorry to bother you, but I need a little help.

Takashi: Sure. What do you want me to do?

Janet: I ①_____ to show me how to make pie charts. I'm not ②_____ using Excel*.

Takashi: Well, it's not so difficult. In fact ③_____ Excel with my sales report now. I'll show you.

Janet: Oh, thank you very much.

Takashi: First, ④_____ data to create a pie chart.

Janet: Uh-huh.

Takashi: Next, select the data that you'd like ⑤_____ in the chart.

Janet: Oh, I ⑥_____. Then, I should click the "Insert" menu on the top tool bar, and select "Chart" from the list ⑦_____.

Takashi: That's right. You have a lot of options to ⑧_____.

*Excel: エクセル（マイクロソフト社が販売している表計算ソフトの名称）

聞き取りのヒント

"Nice to meet you." の meet you が「ミーチュ」のように発音されることはよく知られていますが、この meet や want のように [t] で終わる単語のすぐ後に you のような [j] の音で始まる語が来ると、2つの音が一緒になって [tʃ]「チュ」という別の音に変わってしまいます。こうした現象を「音の同化」と言います。

GRAMMAR 文法に強くなろう！

A. 例にならい、カッコ内に to が必要であれば to を、不要であれば×を書き入れましょう。

   例　I have a lot of reports (to) make.

   1. It looks heavy. Let me (　　　) give you a hand.
   2. I'd like (　　　) pay by credit card.
   3. Would you like (　　　) something to drink?
   4. If you have questions, feel free (　　　) call me anytime.

B. 例にならい枠の中から適切な単語を選び、to 不定詞の形にして次の 1 ～ 4 の文を完成させましょう。

   例　I jog every morning (to stay) healthy.

   1. I was excited (　　　) about your project.
   2. Sorry (　　　) you, but I need to talk to you now.
   3. I want to learn how (　　　) good presentations.
   4. Is Mr. Smith already here? I expected him (　　　) much later.

arrive	hear
make	bother
stay ✓	

C. 日本語の意味に合うようにカッコ内の語句を並び替え、英文を完成させましょう。ただし、文の始めにくる単語も小文字にしてあります。

   1. 上司が今日早退することを許可してくれました。
      My (me / leave / boss / allowed / early / to) today.

   2. オフィスを案内してくださってありがとうございます。
      It is (to / you / kind / show / me / of) around the office.

   3. どこから手をつけたらよいのかわかりません。
      (where / begin / I / don't / know / to).

   4. 忙しくて、テレビを見る時間なんてありません。
      I'm very busy, so I (don't / television / have / to / time / watch).

LET'S READ!

下の説明書を読んで1～3の質問に答えましょう。

Pie Chart

Using spreadsheet software, you can quickly turn your data into a pie chart, and then give that pie chart a professional look. Pie charts are used to show pieces of a whole in relation to each other. They always use one data series.

To create a pie chart in Figure 1, follow Steps 1 to 3.

1. Select the range B4:B7.
2. On the "Insert" tab, in the "Charts" group, choose "Pie."
3. Select the type of pie chart you want.

You can easily change the chart to suit your own needs.

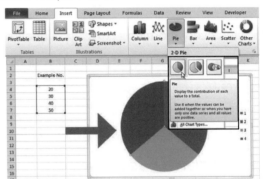

Figure 1.

1. What are the instructions for?
    A. How to print out a pie chart
    B. How to draw a pie graph on a computer
    C. How to create a line graph

2. How many data series do pie charts use?
    A. One
    B. Two
    C. Three

3. What is the final instruction?
    A. On the "Insert" tab, in the "Charts" group, choose "Pie."
    B. Select the type of pie chart you want.
    C. Select the range B4:B7.

NOTES

spreadsheet: 表計算　　in relation to: ～との関連で　　range: 範囲　　suit: ～に合う

CHALLENGE YOURSELF!

リスニングテストで自分の力を試してみましょう。

Part I • Photographs

A～Cの英文を聞いて写真の描写として最も適切なものを選びましょう。

1.

   A   B   C

2.

   A   B   C

Part II • Question-Response

最初に聞こえてくる英文に対する応答として最も適切なものをA～Cの中から選びましょう。

3. A   B   C
4. A   B   C

Part III • Short Conversations

会話を聞き、下の英文が会話の内容とあっていればT（True）、間違っていればF（False）を○で囲みましょう。

5. The man needs three weeks before he decides.   T   F
6. The woman does not know how to use the scanner.   T   F

LET'S READ ALOUD & WRITE! 音読筆写で覚えよう！

授業のまとめとして、今日学習した対話文を3回書き写してしっかり覚えましょう。1度英文を声に出して読んでから書き写すと頭に残りやすくなります。

今日の一言

You're never too old to learn.（学ぶのに遅すぎることは決してない）

UNIT 08 She knows marketing very well.

文法 関係詞 1

タカシとジャネットが話していると、同僚のキャロルのことが話題に上ります。会話では、比較をしたり、意味を確認したりする表現を学びます。また、文法では関係代名詞に焦点を当てて学習します。

WARM-UP 授業前に確認しておこう！

Vocabulary Preview

1～10の語句の意味として適切なものをa～jの中から選びましょう。 CD 37

1. smart　　　　＿＿＿　　　a. (人) と仲良くやる、(人) とよい関係にある
2. suggestion　＿＿＿　　　b. 加わる
3. get along with　＿＿＿　c. 意味する
4. work out　　＿＿＿　　　d. 何とか解決する
5. true　　　　＿＿＿　　　e. 多少の、少しの
6. mean　　　　＿＿＿　　　f. 印象的な、素晴らしい
7. section　　＿＿＿　　　g. 本当の
8. impressive　＿＿＿　　　h. 提案
9. join　　　　＿＿＿　　　i. (会社などの) 部、課
10. a few　　　＿＿＿　　　j. 頭がよい

ビートに乗って1～10の語句を発音してみましょう。

Grammar Point　関係詞1

I met <u>a woman</u> **who** can speak four languages.
（4ヶ国語を話せる女性に会いました）

I have <u>a friend</u> **whose** father is a lawyer.
（私には父親が弁護士をしている友人がいます）

I've lost <u>the file</u> **which** Julia gave me.
（ジュリアがくれたファイルをなくしてしまいました）

「4ヶ国語を話せる女性」のように、下線部分と名詞（この場合は「女性」）をつなぐ（関係づける）働きをするのが**関係代名詞**です。関係代名詞で説明される名詞を**先行詞**と呼びますが、その先行詞が人かそうでないかによって関係代名詞は次の表のような使い分けをします。

先行詞	主格	所有格	目的格
人	who	whose	who / whom
人以外	which	whose	which
人・人以外	that	ー	that

目的格の関係代名詞は省略されることもあります。

1番目の例文は次の2つの文を1つにしたものと考えればよいでしょう。

A. I met <u>a woman</u>.
B. <u>She</u> can speak four languages.

 I met a woman <u>who</u> can speak four languages.

下線部分の a woman と she は同一人物なのでここを関係代名詞でつなぐわけですが、she は元の文の主語なので主格の関係代名詞 who を使います。同様に、3番目の例文は次の2文を1つにしたものです。下線部分の a file と it が同一のものなのでここを関係代名詞でつなぎ、it は元の文の目的語なので目的格の関係代名詞 which を使います。

A. Julia gave me <u>a file</u>.
B. I've lost <u>it</u>.

→ I've lost the file <u>which</u> Julia gave me.

下の例文の日本語訳を完成させながら使い方を確認しましょう。

A consultant is a person <u>who</u> gives advice to people on business.

(コンサルタントとは   )

A firefighter is a person <u>whose</u> job is to stop fires.

(_____)

Is this the file you're looking for?

(これが   )

LET'S LISTEN! 会話の大意を聞き取ろう！

タカシとジャネットの会話を聞いて、質問に対する答えとして最も適切なものを A～C の中から1つ選びましょう。 38

Question 1 When did Carol join Takashi's department?

A. A few weeks ago
B. A month ago
C. A few months ago

Question 2 What does Takashi think of Carol?

A. He enjoys working with her.
B. She's smart but makes very bad suggestions.
C. She's hard to get along with.

Question 3 What does Julia say about Takashi and Carol?

A. They need to discuss their problem.
B. She will take care of their problem.
C. They get along well with each other.

LET'S CHECK & READ ALOUD! 音読してみよう！

1. スクリプトを見ながら会話をもう１度聞き、下線部に当てはまる表現を書き入れましょう。（下線部には単語が２つ入ります）
2. 内容を確認して、全文を音読してみましょう。
3. Takashi と Janet の役割をパートナーと一緒に演じてみましょう。

Janet: I really liked Carol's presentation at the sales meeting. It was so impressive. I don't know anyone ①_____ as much about marketing as she does.

Takashi: Yes, that's true. But we've had a few problems.

Janet: What do you mean?

Takashi: Well, she joined our section a ②_____. She's smart and makes ③_____. But she's difficult to get along with. I don't want to work with her.

Janet: Have you ④_____ her about it?

Takashi: I've ⑤_____, but she just doesn't listen.

Janet: What does Julia say about her?

Takashi: She says I ⑥_____ talk to her again and ⑦_____ out.

Janet: Well, that is a problem. If there is anything I can do to help, just ⑧_____ know.

Takashi: Thanks. I will.

聞き取りのヒント

音読する際には強弱に注意することが大切ですが、強勢を入れて発音することで様々な意味を伝えることができます。例えば対話の中の "Well, that is a problem." という英文では、is に強勢を置いて "Well, that IS a problem." のように発音することで、「それは確かに問題ですね（大変なことね）」という意味を伝えることができます。

GRAMMAR 文法に強くなろう！

A. 次の文の空所に補うのに適切な関係代名詞をカッコ内から選び○で囲みましょう。

1. What's the name of the woman (who / whose / whom) just started working in your office?
2. This is the man (who / whose / that) smartphone has been stolen.
3. Where is the clock (who / whose / that) was hanging on the wall?
4. That's the company (that / who / where) I applied to last year.

B. 例にならい、関係代名詞節を用いて2つの文を1つにまとめましょう。出だしが書いてあるものはそれに続く形で文を作りましょう。

例 Janet gave me a file. I've lost it.
　　I've lost the file Janet gave me.

1. Phil is talking to a woman. Do you know her?
　　_____

2. Janet told us a story. No one believed it.
　　No one _____

3. The website is very useful. You suggested it to me.
　　The website _____

4. I have a friend. Her husband runs a very popular restaurant.
　　_____

C. 日本語の意味に合うようにカッコ内の語句を並び替え、英文を完成させましょう。

1. 昨年オープンしたそのレストランはとても人気があります。
　　The restaurant (last year / which / very / popular / is / opened).
　　_____

2. ジムは僕が先週買ったのと同じカバンを持っています。
　　Jim has (the / briefcase / that / I / bought / same) last week.
　　_____

3. 私の顧客には奥さんが人気女優の人がいます。
　　I have a client (wife / popular / a / actress / is / whose).
　　_____

4. バス停に立っている男性が新しい営業部長ですよ。
　　The man (by / is / standing / the bus stop / who / is) the new sales manager.
　　_____

LET'S READ!

下のメモを読んで1〜3の質問に答えましょう。

To: Takashi, Phil, Carol, and Yoko
From: Julia

Please note that I'll be away for two weeks starting next Wednesday. I'll be attending the national marketing convention in New York for the first five days and then on vacation for the rest. If you have any questions or concerns about our project during my absence, Takashi will be here, so please get in touch with him. If it is an urgent matter, you can still contact me by e-mail. I'll be checking messages every day. Have a great couple of weeks, and I'll see you all when I get back.

Julia

---

1. Why will Julia be away?

    A. For a meeting

    B. For a vacation

    C. For a meeting and a vacation

2. Who will be in charge during Julia's absence?

    A. Yoko

    B. Takashi

    C. Takashi and Yoko

3. What should they do if it is an emergency?

    A. Check messages

    B. Call Julia

    C. Send an e-mail to Julia

NOTES

concern: 懸案事項   absence: 不在、留守   urgent: 緊急の

CHALLENGE YOURSELF!

リスニングテストで自分の力を試してみましょう。

Part I • Photographs

A〜Cの英文を聞いて写真の描写として最も適切なものを選びましょう。

1.

   A B C

2.

   A B C

Part II • Question-Response

最初に聞こえてくる英文に対する応答として最も適切なものをA〜Cの中から選びましょう。

3. A B C

4. A B C

Part III • Short Conversations

会話を聞き、下の英文が会話の内容とあっていればT（True）、間違っていればF（False）を○で囲みましょう。

5. The man will not be able to finish the draft today. T F
6. The woman needs advice about her clients. T F

LET'S READ ALOUD & WRITE! 音読筆写で覚えよう！

授業のまとめとして、今日学習した対話文を3回書き写してしっかり覚えましょう。1度英文を声に出して読んでから書き写すと頭に残りやすくなります。

今日の一言

One who never asks either knows everything or nothing.
（何も質問しない人は、何でも知っているか、何も知らないかのどちらかだ）
Malcolm Stevenson Forbes（1919-1990）

Thank you for coming to our interview.

文法 動名詞

タカシの上司ジュリアのもとにヘッドハンティングの話が舞い込み、ジュリアは面接官のスティーブと会うことにします。会話では、初対面の挨拶や意見を述べる表現を学びます。また、文法では**動名詞**に焦点を当てて学習します。

WARM-UP 授業前に確認しておこう！

Vocabulary Preview

1～10の語句の意味として適切なものをa～jの中から選びましょう。　　CD 42

1. find	_____	a. 責任
2. look forward to	_____	b. 確かに、必ず
3. current	_____	c. 現在の
4. worry	_____	d. やりがいのある、刺激的な
5. pressure	_____	e. ～を楽しみに待つ
6. certainly	_____	f. ～だと感じる、～だとわかる
7. interview	_____	g. （才能・特徴などを）引き出す
8. challenging	_____	h. 面接
9. responsibility	_____	i. 重圧、多忙
10. bring out	_____	j. 心配する

ビートに乗って1～10の語句を発音してみましょう。

Grammar Point 動名詞

　　<u>Seeing</u> is <u>believing</u>. （百聞は一見にしかず）[主語や補語になる]
　　I <u>enjoy meeting</u> new people.
　　　　（私は新しい人々に出会うことを楽しんでいます）[動詞の目的語になる]
　　Thank you for <u>coming</u> all the way here.
　　　　（わざわざこちらまでおいでくださりありがとうございます）[前置詞の目的語になる]

　動詞のing形は「～している」という進行形で使われますが、それとは別に動詞を「～すること」のように名詞化する場合にも使われ、これを**動名詞**と言います。動詞が名詞の働きをするものにはto不定詞もありますが、下の表で、動名詞とto不定詞の注意すべき用法を確認しましょう。

必ず動名詞を目的語とする動詞	enjoy, finish, mind, stop, suggest etc.
必ず to 不定詞を目的語とする動詞	expect, hope, learn, mean, want etc.
どちらも目的語とする動詞	begin, like, love, start etc.

| 動名詞か to 不定詞かで意味が異なる動詞 | forget, remember, try etc.
動名詞は「すでに起きたこと」、to 不定詞は「これから先のこと」と覚えておくとよいでしょう。
ex.) I <u>remember meeting</u> the man.（〜したことを覚えている）
　　 <u>Remember to take</u> your medicine.（忘れずに〜する）|

また、前ページの３番目の例文のように前置詞の後には to 不定詞ではなく必ず動名詞を使います。下の表に挙げる表現では動名詞がよく使われます。

be used to...	〜に慣れている
feel like...	〜したい気がする
How about...?	〜してはどうですか？
Would you mind...?	〜して頂けませんか？

下の例文の日本語訳を完成させながら使い方を確認しましょう。

I look forward to <u>hearing</u> from you.

(　　　　　　　　　　　　　　　　　　　　　　　　　　　　)

How about <u>getting</u> together sometime soon?

(　　　　　　　　　　　　　　　　　　　　　　　　　　　　)

I can't talk right now. Would you mind <u>calling</u> back later?

(　　　　　　　　　　　　　　　　　　　　　　　　　　　　)

LET'S LISTEN! 会話の大意を聞き取ろう！

ジュリアと面接官スティーブの会話を聞いて、質問に対する答えとして最も適切なものをA〜Cの中から１つ選びましょう。 43

Question 1 What does the man ask Julia?

A. How long she has been the sales manager
B. Her current boss
C. Her current salary

Question 2 What does Julia say about her current job?

A. It's not interesting.
B. It's too stressful.
C. It's challenging.

Question 3 What does Julia think of working under pressure?

A. She doesn't worry about it.
B. She doesn't like it.
C. She's worried about it.

LET'S CHECK & READ ALOUD! 音読してみよう！

1. スクリプトを見ながら会話をもう1度聞き、下線部に当てはまる表現を書き入れましょう。（下線部には単語が2つ入ります） 43
2. 内容を確認して、全文を音読してみましょう。
3. Steve と Julia の役割をパートナーと一緒に演じてみましょう。

Steve: Have a seat. Thank you for coming to our interview today.

Julia: Not ①_____. Thank you for inviting me.

Steve: I've been ②_____ to meeting you. I've heard a lot about you.

Julia: Only good things, I hope.

Steve: Of course. Well, let's ③_____ to business. First I'd like to ask you about your ④_____. You've been sales manager for three years now?

Julia: That's right.

Steve: How do you ⑤_____?

Julia: Well, ⑥_____. It has a lot of responsibility, and a lot of pressure. But I don't ⑦_____ under pressure.

Steve: Well, we certainly have a lot of pressure here.

Julia: I wouldn't worry about that. In fact, pressure ⑧_____ the best in me.

音読のヒント

business や position など、カタカナ英語として定着している単語は、「ビジネス」や「ポジション」のように [zi] を「ジ」と読んでしまいがちですが、正しく「ビズィネス」[bíznəs]、「ポズィション」[pəzíʃn] と発音するようにしましょう。同様に、busy や positive も「ビズィ」[bízi]、「ポズィティヴ」[pázitiv] と正しく発音しましょう。

GRAMMAR 文法に強くなろう！

A. 例にならい枠の中から適切な単語を選び、必要な場合は適切な形にして次の1～4の文を完成させましょう。

例 Thank you for (helping) me.

1. You don't have to hurry. I don't mind (   ).
2. Julia wants (   ) the meeting.
3. I'm not good at (   ) pictures.
4. Carol left without (   ) goodbye.

```
draw     say
cancel   wait
help ✓
```

B. 例にならいカッコ内から正しい語句を選び○で囲みましょう。

例 How about ((going)/ go) out for dinner?

1. I'm looking forward to (work / working) with you again.
2. Do you really enjoy (to work / working) here?
3. We hope (to see / seeing) you there.
4. There used to (be / being) a big park over there.

C. 日本語の意味に合うようにカッコ内の語句を並び替え、英文を完成させましょう。ただし、文の始めにくる単語も小文字にしてあります。

1. 昨日電話できなくてすみません。

    I'm (for / you / not / yesterday / sorry / calling).

    _____

2. ご連絡をお待ちしております。

    (to / hear / we / you / from / hope) soon.

    _____

3. 英語でメールを書くことにだんだん慣れてきたところです。

    (I'm / to / getting / e-mails / writing / used) in English.

    _____

4. 忘れずに彼女に電話をかけ直してくださいね。

    (forget / to / her / don't / back / call).

    _____

LET'S READ!

次のパッセージを読んで1～3の質問に答えましょう。

First Impressions

Job interviews are challenging and few people look forward to them. But with a little practice, you can certainly succeed. Here are a few pieces of advice.

- Dress well. Wearing a good suit will help to create a positive first impression.
- Thinking carefully about your body language and practicing your interview with a friend will help you to stay calm under pressure.
- Finally, "by failing to prepare, you are preparing to fail!" Asking good questions and showing interest in the company is very important, so learn as much as you can about the company's business. Above all, don't worry! Good luck!

1. The comment that "few people look forward to them" suggests that job interviews are very _____.
    A. enjoyable
    B. stressful
    C. successful

2. The comment that "Wearing a good suit will help to create a positive first impression" means that interviewers will notice your _____.
    A. appearance
    B. friend
    C. skirt

3. The most important advice is that you should _____.
    A. talk as much as you can
    B. prepare to fail
    C. prepare well for the interview

NOTES

impression: 印象　　calm: 落ち着いて　　above all: 何にもまして　　notice: 気づく

CHALLENGE YOURSELF!

リスニングテストで自分の力を試してみましょう。

Part I • Photographs

A〜Cの英文を聞いて写真の描写として最も適切なものを選びましょう。 44

1.

A   B   C

2.

A   B   C

Part II • Question-Response

最初に聞こえてくる英文に対する応答として最も適切なものをA〜Cの中から選びましょう。 45

3.　A　　B　　C

4.　A　　B　　C

Part III • Short Conversations

会話を聞き、下の英文が会話の内容とあっていればT（True）、間違っていればF（False）を○で囲みましょう。 46

5. The man's wallet was stolen.　　　　　　　　　　　　　　T　　F

6. The man has left his glasses on his desk.　　　　　　T　　F

LET'S READ ALOUD & WRITE! 音読筆写で覚えよう！

授業のまとめとして、今日学習した対話文を3回書き写してしっかり覚えましょう。1度英文を声に出して読んでから書き写すと頭に残りやすくなります。

今日の一言

It is no use crying over spilt milk.（覆水盆に返らず）

UNIT 10 The competition will be very strong.

文法 形容詞・副詞

販売会議の場でジュリア、タカシ、キャロルたちが今後の販売戦略について話し合っています。会話では、意見を求めたり、理解を示したりする表現を学びます。また、文法では**形容詞・副詞**に焦点を当てて学習します。

WARM-UP 授業前に確認しておこう！

Vocabulary Preview

1〜10の語句の意味として適切なものを a〜j の中から選びましょう。　CD 47

1. budget　　＿＿＿＿＿
2. update　　＿＿＿＿＿
3. agree　　＿＿＿＿＿
4. limited　　＿＿＿＿＿
5. competitor　　＿＿＿＿＿
6. consider　　＿＿＿＿＿
7. similar　　＿＿＿＿＿
8. exactly　　＿＿＿＿＿
9. regularly　　＿＿＿＿＿
10. impact　　＿＿＿＿＿

a. 似たような、類似の
b. （相づちとして）まさにその通りです
c. 競争相手、ライバル
d. 影響、効果
e. 最新の状態にする、更新する
f. 限りがある
g. 同意する
h. 検討する
i. 定期的に
j. 予算

ビートに乗って 1〜10 の語句を発音してみましょう。

Grammar Point　形容詞・副詞

I need <u>a few</u> days to finish this report.　［ a few ➡ （数について）少しはある ］
（この報告書を仕上げるのに数日必要だ）

There were <u>few</u> mistakes in his report.　［ few ➡ （数について）ほとんどない ］
（彼の報告書には間違いがほとんどなかった）

We still have <u>a little</u> time left, so let's finish this today.　［ a little ➡ （量について）少しはある ］
（時間がまだ少しあるから、これを今日済ませてしまおう）

We have <u>little</u> time today, so let's discuss it tomorrow.　［ little ➡ （量について）ほとんどない ］
（今日はほとんど時間がないから、明日それを話し合いましょう）

　形容詞は、a happy day における happy のように、**名詞と結びついて人やものの状態や性質を説明するもの**です。形容詞は基本的に名詞の直前に置かれる他、"She looks happy." のように、動詞の後に置いて主語（＝名詞・代名詞）に説明を加えたりします。それに対し、**副詞**は、"She sang happily." における happily のように、動詞や形容詞、他の副詞といった**名詞以外のものと結びついて様子や場所、時、頻度などを説明するもの**です。次の表で副詞の種類を確認しましょう。

様態	どのように	well / fast など	Julia checked the report **carefully**.	
場所	どこで	here / home など	I came **home** late last night.	
時	いつ	late / soon など	You should call your client **soon**.	
頻度	どれくらい の度合いで	always / often など	I **usually** drive to work, but today I took the bus. Kate is **never** late for meetings.	
程度	どれだけ	almost / hardly など	I **almost** forgot.	

（一般動詞の前、be動詞・助動詞の後に置くのが基本。）

（修飾する語句の直前が基本。ただし動詞を修飾する場合は一般動詞の前、be動詞・助動詞の後に置きます。）

　一般に、副詞は carefully や strongly のように -ly で終わるものが多いですが、hard（懸命に）と hardly（ほとんど～でない）、late（遅れて）と lately（最近）のように、似た副詞で意味の異なるものがあります。また、early（形早い／副早く）、well（形健康な／副うまく）、pretty（形かわいい／副かなり）など、形容詞と副詞が同じ形のものもあるので要注意です。

　下の例文の日本語訳を完成させながら使い方を確認しましょう。

I hear Carol works very <u>hard</u>, but I've only met her once. I <u>hardly</u> know her.

（　　　　　　　　　　　　　　　　　　　　　　　　　　　　　　　　　）

I've been really busy <u>lately</u>, so I come home very <u>late</u> at night.

（　　　　　　　　　　　　　　　　　　　　　　　　　　　　　　　　　）

Julia's daughter is very <u>pretty</u> and sings <u>pretty</u> well, too.

（　　　　　　　　　　　　　　　　　　　　　　　　　　　　　　　　　）

LET'S LISTEN!　会話の大意を聞き取ろう！

タカシとジュリア、キャロルの会話を聞いて、質問に対する答えとして最も適切なものをA～Cの中から1つ選びましょう。 48

Question 1　What is said about this year's sales?

　A. They will increase by five percent.
　B. They will slow down.
　C. They will go down quickly.

Question 2　What does Takashi say about the current market?

　A. There are few competitors.
　B. There are only a few competitors.
　C. There are many competitors.

Question 3　What is said about TV commercials?

　A. People don't watch them.
　B. They have little impact on people.
　C. They cost a lot of money.

LET'S CHECK & READ ALOUD! 音読してみよう！

1. スクリプトを見ながら会話をもう1度聞き、下線部に当てはまる表現を書き入れましょう。（下線部には単語が2つ入ります） 48
2. 内容を確認して、全文を音読してみましょう。
3. Takashi と Julia & Carol（1人2役）の役割をパートナーと一緒に演じてみましょう。

Julia: Last year we had a five-percent increase in sales. But they're expected to ①_____ this year.

Takashi: That's right. There were ②_____ three years ago, but now there are a lot of ③_____.

Julia: Exactly. What can we do to improve sales?

Takashi: Of course, we'll ④_____ update our website regularly. But we have to ⑤_____ ways, too.

Julia: I agree. What other media should we use?

Takashi: What do you ⑥_____ ads in newspapers?

Carol: Do people really read the ads in newspapers? I don't.

Takashi: Then, how about TV commercials?

Carol: TV is ⑦_____ the question. It's too expensive.

Takashi: But if they are good, they'll have an impact.

Julia: Well, I see ⑧_____. The problem is our budget is quite limited.

聞き取りのヒント

会話の中で使われていた a lot of や out of は、それぞれ「アロロヴ」、「アウロヴ」のように聞こえます。音がつながるだけなら「アロトヴ」、「アウトヴ」になりそうですが、アメリカ英語では [t] が母音に挟まれた場合、ラ行に近い音になります。better [bétər] なども、アメリカ人が発音すると「ベラー」のように聞こえます。

GRAMMAR 文法に強くなろう！

A. 例にならい枠の中から適切な単語を選んで次の1～4の文を完成させましょう。

　例　"I was wrong. I apologize." "(Never) mind."

　1. I'm still sleepy. I didn't sleep (　　　　) last night.
　2. It's raining (　　　　) now.
　3. I (　　　　) finish work at five, but I worked overtime yesterday.
　4. My vacation is (　　　　) over. I have to go back to work tomorrow.

heavily	usually
almost	well
never ✓	

B. 例にならいカッコ内から正しい語句を選び○で囲みましょう。

　例　Please be ((quiet)/ quietly). I'm talking on the phone now.

　1. Your French is very (good / well). You speak it very (good / well).
　2. Kate is working (hard / hardly) for her presentation tomorrow.
　3. You look (sad / sadly). What's the matter?
　4. I've made a (careful / carefully) plan for the new project.

C. 日本語の意味に合うようにカッコ内の語句を並び替え、英文を完成させましょう。ただし、文の始めにくる単語も小文字にしてあります。

　1. 音声は聞こえますか？ 十分な大きさですか？
　　Can you hear the sound? (enough / for / is / you / it / loud)?
　　_____

　2. とても忙しくて今日中にすべてのファイルを確認することはできません。
　　I'm (that / check / can't / busy / I / so) all the files today.
　　_____

　3. 週末が待ち遠しいです。
　　I (wait / the / weekend / can / hardly / till).
　　_____

　4. オフィスには人はほとんどいませんでした。
　　(there / people / in / few / the / were) office.
　　_____

LET'S READ!

下のメモを読んで1〜3の質問に答えましょう。

> To: Takashi, Janet, Phil, and Yoko
> From: Julia
>
> Hi everyone,
> I wanted to give you an update about our competitor's sales report.
> As you know, their early year results were pretty good, then they had a sharp drop in spring after their problems became public. Since then they've been slowly recovering, but we should definitely try to improve our sales while their position is weak. Our own situation isn't great, but if we use our budget wisely, and plan carefully, we can certainly make a big impact over the next year.
> Please consider what we can do to make our position stronger. I expect suggestions from everyone.
>
> Julia

1. The year started _____ for the rival company.

    A. badly

    B. slowly

    C. well

2. Which statement is correct?

    A. Julia says that if they spend a lot of money, they can sell more than their rivals.

    B. Julia wants to gain an advantage over the rival company.

    C. Julia's company is in a strong position.

3. Julia wants everyone to give her some good _____.

    A. ideas

    B. money

    C. position

NOTES

update: 最新情報　　public: 公に　　recover: 回復する　　wisely: 賢く

CHALLENGE YOURSELF!

リスニングテストで自分の力を試してみましょう。

Part I • Photographs

A～Cの英文を聞いて写真の描写として最も適切なものを選びましょう。

1.

    A B C

2.

    A B C

Part II • Question-Response

最初に聞こえてくる英文に対する応答として最も適切なものをA～Cの中から選びましょう。

3. A B C

4. A B C

Part III • Short Conversations

会話を聞き、下の英文が会話の内容とあっていればT（True）、間違っていればF（False）を○で囲みましょう。

5. The man is busy preparing for tomorrow's meeting. T F
6. The man wants the minutes of the meeting today. T F

LET'S READ ALOUD & WRITE! 音読筆写で覚えよう！

授業のまとめとして、今日学習した対話文を3回書き写してしっかり覚えましょう。1度英文を声に出して読んでから書き写すと頭に残りやすくなります。

今日の一言

Opportunity seldom knocks twice.（好機はめったに2度訪れない）

UNIT 11　This is where we hold meetings.

文法　関係詞2

いよいよプレゼンの日がやってきました。当日タカシは少し早目に取引先のサリーを訪ね、準備をします。会話では、人を案内したり、提案したりする表現を学びます。また、文法では**関係代名詞と関係副詞**に焦点を当てて学習します。

WARM-UP　授業前に確認しておこう！

Vocabulary Preview

1～10の語句の意味として適切なものを a～j の中から選びましょう。　　　 52

1. check out　　＿＿＿　　a. 配布資料
2. connect　　　＿＿＿　　b. コピーする
3. handout　　　＿＿＿　　c. 映写機、投影機
4. early　　　　＿＿＿　　d. 念のため
5. follow　　　　＿＿＿　　e. ～をよく調べる、～を調査する
6. here you are　＿＿＿　　f. 予行演習をする
7. projector　　　＿＿＿　　g. ～を接続する
8. make a copy　＿＿＿　　h. （定刻より）早い
9. just in case　　＿＿＿　　i. ～の後について行く
10. rehearse　　　＿＿＿　　j. はいどうぞ

ビートに乗って1～10の語句を発音してみましょう。

Grammar Point　関係詞2

The president has two sons, **who** work in his company.
　　（社長には息子が2人いるが、その息子たちは彼の会社で働いている）［継続用法］
The president has two sons **who** work in his company.
　　（社長には彼の会社で働いている2人の息子がいる）［限定用法］
You've been working too hard. **What** you need is some rest.
　　（君は働き過ぎだよ。君に必要なのは少し休むことだ）
This is <u>the bank</u> <u>**where** my father works</u>.（ここが父の働いている銀行です）

　関係代名詞についてはすでに触れましたが、関係代名詞にはその前にカンマ（,）がつくパターンがあり、**継続用法**や**非限定用法**と呼ばれます。上の1番目の例文では、社長には2人の息子がいて、カンマ以下ではその息子に関する補足説明をしています。それに対し、カンマのつかない2番目の例文では、「彼の会社で働いている2人の息子」のように限定していますので、**限定用法**と呼ばれます。この場合、彼の会社で働いていない子どもも存在する可能性があります。また、3番目の例文にある

what は "the thing(s) which..."（～するもの・こと）のように先行詞を含む関係代名詞ですから、who や which などとは使い方を区別しておく必要があります。

　この他、関係代名詞と似た働きをするものに**関係副詞**があります。4 番目の例文は次の 2 つの文を 1 つにしたものと考えればよいでしょう。

　　A. This is <u>the bank</u>.
　　B. My father works <u>there</u>. This is the bank <u>where</u> my father works.

　下線部分の there は at the bank と言い換えられますので、場所を示す関係副詞 where を使うのです。関係代名詞 which を使って、"This is the bank <u>at which</u> my father works." と言うことも可能です。関係副詞には where の他にも下の表に挙げるものがあります。

先行詞	場所を表す語	時を表す語	reason(s)	なし
関係副詞	where	when	why	how

　下の例文の日本語訳を完成させながら使い方を確認しましょう。

My sister Jane, <u>who</u> is a nurse, lives in London.

　　(　　　　　　　　　　　　　　　　　　　　　　　　　　　　)

This is just <u>what</u> I needed.

　　(　　　　　　　　　　　　　　　　　　　　　　　　　　　　)

This is the office <u>where</u> I work.

　　(　　　　　　　　　　　　　　　　　　　　　　　　　　　　)

LET'S LISTEN!　会話の大意を聞き取ろう！

タカシとサリーの会話を聞いて、質問に対する答えとして最も適切なものを A～C の中から 1 つ選びましょう。 53

Question 1　Which computer is Takashi probably going to use?

　A. His own computer
　B. Sally's computer
　C. The one which is already connected to the projector

Question 2　How many people are going to attend the meeting?

　A. About 15
　B. About 20
　C. About 50

Question 3　What does Sally offer to do?

　A. Watch him rehearse his presentation
　B. Connect his computer to the projector
　C. Make copies of his handout

LET'S CHECK & READ ALOUD! 音読してみよう！

1. スクリプトを見ながら会話をもう1度聞き、下線部に当てはまる表現を書き入れましょう。（下線部には単語が2つ入ります） 53
2. 内容を確認して、全文を音読してみましょう。
3. Takashi と Sally の役割をパートナーと一緒に演じてみましょう。

Sally: Hi, Takashi. Good to see you. You're ①_____!

Takashi: Good to see you too, Sally. I know I'm a little early, but I ②_____ check out the room before my presentation.

Sally: Oh, I see. Let me ③_____ to the meeting room. Follow me. This is ④_____ going to make your presentation today.

Takashi: I see. Can I rehearse my presentation here?

Sally: Of course. You can use this computer, ⑤_____ already connected to the projector.

Takashi: Thanks. The data is in this memory stick. By the way, how many people are going to be at the meeting?

Sally: About 15. Would you like me to ⑥_____ of your handout?

Takashi: That ⑦_____ great. This is the handout. Here you are.

Sally: OK. I'll make ⑧_____ just in case.

聞き取りのヒント

音の同化についてはすでに触れましたが、[k] の子音で終わる単語の後に、you [juː] などのように [j] の音で始まる語が来たときも、やはり発音が少しわかりにくくなります。例えば、take you は「テイクユー」ではなく「テイキュ」のように、make your は「メイクユア」ではなく「メイキョア」のように、日本語の拗音（「キャ」などの小さなゃ）に似た音になります。

GRAMMAR 文法に強くなろう！

A. 次の文の空所に補うのに適切な関係詞をカッコ内から選び○で囲みましょう。

1. Here's a map of the town (which / where / whose) we're going.
2. This is the reason (where / why / when) I gave up my job.
3. That's not (what / which / that) I said.
4. I forgot the year (where / what / when) my father was born.

B. 日本語と同じ意味になるように、AとBのうち適切な方を選んで○で囲みましょう。

1. 私のオフィスは2階にあるのですが、とても小さいです。
    A: My office, which is on the second floor, is very small.
    B: My office which is on the second floor is very small.
2. スペイン語を話せる人を誰か知っていますか？
    A: Do you know anyone who can speak Spanish?
    B: Do you know anyone, who can speak Spanish?
3. サリーは4ヶ国語を話せるのですが、以前は旅行社に勤めていました。
    A: Sally who can speak four languages worked for a travel company.
    B: Sally, who can speak four languages, worked for a travel company.
4. 妻はニューヨーク在住なのですが、毎日メールを送ってくれます。
    A: My wife who lives in New York sends me e-mails every day.
    B: My wife, who lives in New York, sends me e-mails every day.

C. 日本語の意味に合うようにカッコ内の語句を並び替え、英文を完成させましょう。ただし、文の始めにくる単語も小文字にしてあります。

1. ここが私の以前働いていたオフィスです。
    This is (office / where / used to / the / work / I).
    _____

2. ルークの言うことは信じられません。
    (Luke / I / says / can't / what / believe).
    _____

3. 私には2人姉がいるのですが、2人共同じ会社に勤めています。
    I have two sisters, (work / the / company / same / for / who).
    _____

4. 歯医者に行かないといけませんでした。だから昨日早退したのです。
    I had to go to the dentist. (why / I / early / that's / left) yesterday.
    _____

LET'S READ!

次のパッセージを読んで1～3の質問に答えましょう。

Japanese English

Sally offered to make copies of Takashi's handout. In Japanese, people say "print" (プリント) instead of "handout," but in English, "print" is usually used as a verb, not a noun. Japanese English is often completely different from its original meaning. Do you know what a "mansion" (マンション) is in English? It's a very large, impressive house. Native English speakers will understand "Viking" (バイキング) but will imagine a Scandinavian warrior, not a buffet-style dinner. In Japan, English can be a foreign language, even to native English speakers!

1. Which statement is correct?

    A. "To print" means "to give someone a piece of paper."

    B. A handout is a printed document.

    C. The meaning of "print" is the same in Japanese and English.

2. In English, a mansion means _____.

    A. a building with only one floor

    B. a very large house

    C. an apartment

3. Which statement is correct?

    A. "Viking" means a buffet dinner in English.

    B. "Viking" is a Scandinavian restaurant.

    C. "Viking" is an example of Japanese English.

NOTES

verb: 動詞　　　　**noun:** 名詞　　　　**Scandinavian:** スカンジナビア半島の

buffet: ビュッフェ、セルフサービス式の食事

CHALLENGE YOURSELF!

リスニングテストで自分の力を試してみましょう。

Part I • Photographs

A〜Cの英文を聞いて写真の描写として最も適切なものを選びましょう。

1. A   B   C

2. A   B   C

Part II • Question-Response

最初に聞こえてくる英文に対する応答として最も適切なものをA〜Cの中から選びましょう。

3. A   B   C
4. A   B   C

Part III • Short Conversations

会話を聞き、下の英文が会話の内容とあっていればT（True）、間違っていればF（False）を○で囲みましょう。

5. The man usually works from nine to five.　　　T　F
6. The man is ordering a coffee at a restaurant.　T　F

LET'S READ ALOUD & WRITE! 音読筆写で覚えよう！

授業のまとめとして、今日学習した対話文を3回書き写してしっかり覚えましょう。1度英文を声に出して読んでから書き写すと頭に残りやすくなります。

今日の一言

Don't put off till tomorrow what you can do today.
（今日できることは明日に延ばすな）

UNIT 12 I'd like to talk about our latest model.

文法 分詞

タカシは取引先で主力商品である Alpha シリーズの最新モデル Alpha 7 についてプレゼンをします。会話では、順序を示したり、重点を強調したりする表現を学びます。また、文法では**分詞**に焦点を当てて学習します。

WARM-UP 授業前に確認しておこう！

Vocabulary Preview

1〜10の語句の意味として適切なものをa〜jの中から選びましょう。　CD 57

1. improve	_____	a. 革新者
2. explain	_____	b. 市場占有率、シェア
3. successful	_____	c. 洗練された
4. feature	_____	d. 全世界の、国際的な
5. share	_____	e. 成功した
6. global	_____	f. 説明する
7. promise	_____	g. 改良する
8. latest	_____	h. 最新の
9. stylish	_____	i. 約束する
10. innovator	_____	j. 特徴

ビートに乗って1〜10の語句を発音してみましょう。

Grammar Point　分詞

Who is the man talking with Julia?
　　　　　　（ジュリアと話している男性は誰ですか？）[現在分詞]
The wallet stolen at the airport was found yesterday, but there was nothing in it.
　　　　　　（空港で盗まれた財布は昨日見つかったが、中には何もなかった）[過去分詞]

　分詞には**現在分詞**と**過去分詞**があり、これらは形容詞として使うことができます。上の例文のように、**現在分詞は「〜している」という能動的な意味、過去分詞は「〜された」という受動的な意味**になります。

　形容詞には分詞から派生しているものがあり、exciting / excited のように、感情を表す動詞から派生しているものは使い分けに注意が必要です。exciting と excited はもともと動詞 excite（「(人を) 興奮させる」）のそれぞれ現在分詞、過去分詞なので、exciting は「(人を) 興奮させるような」という能動の意味、excited は「興奮させられた (⇒ 興奮した)」という受動の意味を持ちます。次の表でそうした形容詞の使い方を確認しましょう。

	物や事がどのようなものかを説明する			人がどのように感じたかを説明する	
-ing	My job is	boring. （退屈な） exciting. （刺激的な） interesting. （面白い）	-ed	I'm	bored. （退屈している） excited. （興奮している） interested. （興味を持っている）

分詞の導く句が副詞のように使われ、文の情報を補足します。「～しながら、～なので、～して、～するとき」などの意味を表します。

また、分詞の用法は下の表のように大きく３つに分けられます。

名詞を修飾する （限定用法）	I'd like some <u>iced</u> tea. Do you know the man <u>standing</u> there?
補語となる （叙述用法）	Carol kept me <u>waiting</u> for an hour. I want this file <u>checked</u> right now.
分詞構文	<u>Written</u> in simple English, this report is easy to understand.

１語の場合は名詞の前に置き、他の語句が加わると名詞の後に置きます。

下の例文の日本語訳を完成させながら使い方を確認しましょう。

I don't want to go out with John. He's really **boring**.

(　　　　　　　　　　　　　　　　　　　　　　　　　　　　　　)

Don't leave the door **unlocked**.

(　　　　　　　　　　　　　　　　　　　　　　　　　　　　　　)

I walk to the office every day **listening** to music.

(　　　　　　　　　　　　　　　　　　　　　　　　　　　　　　)

LET'S LISTEN!　会話の大意を聞き取ろう！

タカシのプレゼンを聞いて、質問に対する答えとして最も適切なものをA～Cの中から１つ選びましょう。　　🎧 58

Question 1　How many Alpha series units have been sold so far?

　A. Close to a million
　B. One million
　C. Three million

Question 2　How many features does Takashi mention about Alpha 7?

　A. Two
　B. Three
　C. Seven

Question 3　What is one of the key features of Alpha 7?

　A. Large display
　B. Light weight
　C. Long battery life

LET'S CHECK & READ ALOUD! 音読してみよう！

1. スクリプトを見ながらプレゼンテーションをもう1度聞き、下線部に当てはまる表現を書き入れましょう。（下線部には単語が2つ入ります）
2. 内容を確認して、全文を音読してみましょう。
3. Takashi の役割を各自で演じてみましょう。

Takashi

Hello, everyone. Today ①_____ to talk about our ②_____, Alpha 7.

First, I'll show you our ③_____ in the global market of smart watches.

Next, I'll explain the concept and ④_____ of Alpha 7.

Now, as you know, the Alpha series ⑤_____ very successful with a total of one million units ⑥_____ the past three years.

As you can see from the chart on this slide, the Alpha series has been the leader in the market.

Being a leader ⑦_____ an innovator.

I can promise you that Alpha 7 is an innovative product with three key features: ultrathin body, ⑧_____, and improved battery life.

音読のヒント

the Alpha series の the をつい「ザ」[ðə] と言ってしまうかもしれませんが、母音で始まる単語の前にある the は「ジ」[ði] と発音します。ただし、unit のように、母音字 u で始まっていても実際の発音が母音で始まらない場合は「ザ」と発音します。例：the unit [ðə júːnit]

GRAMMAR 文法に強くなろう！

A. 例にならい枠の中から適切な単語を選び、現在分詞か過去分詞にして次の1～4の文を完成させましょう。

例 Beth kept (*crying*) in front of her father's grave.

feel	steal
make	unlock
cry ✓	

1. Do you know the woman (　　　　) a speech now?
2. The police found the (　　　　) wallet at the airport.
3. Don't keep the door (　　　　).
4. (　　　　) tired, I went to bed early.

B. 例にならいカッコ内から正しい語句を選び○で囲みましょう。

例 Look. I have an ((interesting) / interested) story to tell.

1. I saw a traffic accident yesterday. It was a very (shocked / shocking) experience.
2. Julia's speech was too long and everyone was (boring / bored).
3. We are very (exciting / excited) to attend this year's conference.
4. Can you make yourself (understanding / understood) in English?

C. 日本語の意味に合うようにカッコ内の語句を並び替え、英文を完成させましょう。ただし、文の始めにくる単語も小文字にしてあります。

1. ウェブサイトは常に最新の状態にしておく必要があります。
   We (website / to / updated / our / keep / need).
   _____

2. 誰かがドアをノックするのが聞こえた。
   I (heard / the / knocking / on / door / someone).
   _____

3. 待たせてしまってごめんなさい。
   (sorry / keep / I'm / waiting / you / to).
   _____

4. 私は駅で自分の名前が呼ばれたと思った。
   I (I / name / heard / called / my / thought) at the station.
   _____

LET'S READ!

次のパッセージを読んで1〜3の質問に答えましょう。

Giving a Presentation

The original meaning of "presentation" comes from the Latin, *praesentare*, which means "to be before" or "in front of..." You can see "pre" (meaning "before") in other English words of Latin origin, such as "prepare," "preview" and "prevent." So if you present something, what you have is placed in front of someone. We also use "to present" in another way, meaning "to formally give a gift." However, in informal situations, we use "give." Don't say "I presented a souvenir to my mother." This sounds very formal! It would be much more natural to say "I gave a souvenir to my mother."

1. "Pre-" means "_____."

    A. after

    B. before

    C. original

2. When we present something, we are _____.

    A. preparing it for someone

    B. placing it in front of someone

    C. telling them about Latin words

3. Which is most natural?

    A. I gave my mother some flowers for her birthday.

    B. I placed some flowers to my mother for her birthday.

    C. I presented my mother some flowers for her birthday.

NOTES

Latin: ラテン語　　*praesentare*: プレゼンタレ　　souvenir: お土産　　formal: 堅苦しい

CHALLENGE YOURSELF!

リスニングテストで自分の力を試してみましょう。

Part I • Photographs

A～Cの英文を聞いて写真の描写として最も適切なものを選びましょう。

1.

2.

    A   B   C   A   B   C

Part II • Question-Response

最初に聞こえてくる英文に対する応答として最も適切なものをA～Cの中から選びましょう。

3.   A   B   C

4.   A   B   C

Part III • Short Conversations

会話を聞き、下の英文が会話の内容とあっていればT（True）、間違っていればF（False）を○で囲みましょう。

5. The man doesn't know why the meeting was canceled.   T   F

6. They are talking about the new manager.   T   F

LET'S READ ALOUD & WRITE! 音読筆写で覚えよう！

授業のまとめとして、今日学習した対話文を3回書き写してしっかり覚えましょう。1度英文を声に出して読んでから書き写すと頭に残りやすくなります。

今日の一言

Let sleeping dogs lie.（触らぬ神に祟りなし）

UNIT 13 You are much better than me.

文法 比較

タカシのプレゼンが無事終了した後、同僚のキャロルがタカシのところにやってきます。会話では、感想を述べたり、比較したりする表現を学びます。また、文法では比較に焦点を当てて学習します。

WARM-UP 授業前に確認しておこう！

Vocabulary Preview

1～10の語句の意味として適切なものをa～jの中から選びましょう。 CD 62

1. impressed _____　　a. 驚いた
2. surprised _____　　b. 少しの間、ちょっと
3. admit _____　　c. 競争相手
4. rival _____　　d. まったくわからない
5. have no idea _____　　e. 感動した
6. vice president _____　　f. 辞める
7. quit _____　　g. 競争する
8. compete _____　　h. 有名な
9. for a second _____　　i. 副社長
10. famous _____　　j. 認める

ビートに乗って1～10の語句を発音してみましょう。

Grammar Point　比較

Our president is <u>not as</u> old <u>as</u> he looks. In fact, he's much <u>younger than</u> he looks.
（社長は見た目ほど年取ってはいません。実際見た目よりだいぶ若いです）
<u>More and more</u> companies are globalizing their production bases.
（ますます多くの企業が生産拠点を国際化しつつあります）
We are one of <u>the largest</u> retailers in the world. （当社は世界最大の小売業者の1つです）

形容詞や副詞を使って「～と同じくらい…だ」と2つのものを比較する場合、《as＋形容詞／副詞＋as...》という形で表します。

1音節	2音節	3音節
-er		more ～
-est		most ～

また、「～より大きい」や「最も大きい」のように、他と比較しながら話す場合、「大きい」という形容詞の**比較級**や**最上級**を使って表現します。比較級や最上級にするには、「**1音節の短い単語は語尾に -er（比較級）、-est（最上級）をつけ、3音節以上の長い単語は前に more、most をつける**」が基本ですが、2音節の単語は両方のパターンがあります。また、不規則に変化するものも多くあります。次の表を完成させながら確認しましょう。

		原級	比較級	最上級	
1音節	基本パターン	high	higher	highest	語尾に er / est
	-e で終わる単語	large	larger	largest	語尾に r / st
	〈1母音字＋1子音字〉で終わる単語	big			子音字を重ねて er / est
2音節	〈子音字＋y〉で終わる単語	early	earlier	earliest	y を i に変え er / est
	-er, -le, -ow で終わる単語	simple	simpler	simplest	語尾に er / est
	形容詞に -ly がついた副詞	slowly	more slowly	most slowly	前に more / most
3音節以上		difficult	more difficult	most difficult	
例外的な単語		many	more	most	不規則な変化をする
		good / well			
		little			
		bad			

下の例文の日本語訳を完成させながら使い方を確認しましょう。

This product isn't as popular as it used to be.

(_____)

"Can we schedule a meeting at three?" "Actually, a little earlier might be better. How about two?"

(_____)

Canada is the second largest country in the world after Russia.

(_____)

LET'S LISTEN! 会話の大意を聞き取ろう！

タカシとキャロルの会話を聞いて、質問に対する答えとして最も適切なものを A〜C の中から1つ選びましょう。 63

Question 1 What does Carol say about Takashi's presentation?

A. It was full of mistakes.
B. It was as good as hers.
C. It was really good.

Question 2 What does Carol suggest?

A. Takashi should move to the New York office.
B. Takashi should be the next sales manager.
C. Takashi should compete against Julia.

Question 3 What does Carol say about Julia?

A. She will become the next president.
B. She will leave the company.
C. She will start her own business in New York.

LET'S CHECK & READ ALOUD! 音読してみよう！

1. スクリプトを見ながら会話をもう1度聞き、下線部に当てはまる表現を書き入れましょう。（下線部には単語が2つ入ります） 63
2. 内容を確認して、全文を音読してみましょう。
3. Takashi と Carol の役割をパートナーと一緒に演じてみましょう。

Carol: Hello, Takashi. Can I talk to you for a second?

Takashi: Sure. ①_____?

Carol: Well, I just wanted to ②_____ know that your presentation was great. I ③_____.

Takashi: Oh, thank you. I'm surprised.

Carol: Surprised? Why?

Takashi: You never talked to me.

Carol: Well, I must ④_____. I thought you were my rival and I was ⑤_____ you. But I was wrong. You're much better than me.

Takashi: No, I'm not.

Carol: Yes, you are. You're the ⑥_____ for the next sales manager.

Takashi: Next sales manager? What do you mean?

Carol: Didn't you know that Julia ⑦_____? They say she'll become ⑧_____ of a famous company in New York!

Takashi: I had no idea. I'm really surprised!

音読のヒント

会話の中で使われていた "Didn't you know that...?" の that のように、「～ということ」という接続詞の that は読む際に強勢を取らず、弱く [ðət] と発音します。また、ポーズを取るときはその前で取ります。例えば、"I think that it's too expensive." という文を読む際にどこかで息つぎをするとすれば、I think と that の間となります。実際には I think that の後で切ることもありますが、その場合は次に何を言おうか言葉に詰まって考えているときです。

GRAMMAR 文法に強くなろう！

A. 例にならい空所に下線部の単語の比較級か最上級を入れて次の1～4の文を完成させましょう。

例　I don't speak English very well. You speak it (*better*) than me.

1. I can't type very fast. You type (　　　　) than me.
2. David is very boring. He is the (　　　　) person I've ever met.
3. It was a very bad mistake. It was the (　　　　) mistake I've ever made.
4. The restaurant was expensive. It was (　　　　) than I expected.

B. 例にならいカッコ内から正しい語句を選び○で囲みましょう。

例　This year's market share is ((higher) / highest) than last year's.

1. The new meeting room is (two / twice) as large as the old one.
2. Dave is the youngest (in / of) all the managers.
3. Laura is the same age (as / than) Betty.
4. Quality is (very / much) more important than quantity.

C. 日本語の意味に合うようにカッコ内の語句を並び替え、英文を完成させましょう。ただし、文の始めにくる単語も小文字にしてあります。

1. マーケティングはビジネスにおいて最も重要な活動の1つです。

   Marketing is (important / of / activities / one / the / most) in business.

   _____

2. 最新モデルは以前のモデルほど値段が高くない。

   The latest model (as / older / the / expensive / as / isn't) model.

   _____

3. 今の仕事は好きではありません。もっと面白いことをしてみたいのです。

   I don't like my current job. I (interesting / do / to / more / something / want).

   _____

4. これは今までに見た中で最高の映画です。

   This is (seen / movie / best / ever / the / I've).

   _____

LET'S READ!

ジュリアがタカシに送った電子メールを読んで1～3の質問に答えましょう。

> Dear Takashi,
>
> Sorry to let you know by e-mail, but—as you may have already heard—I'll be leaving to take up a new position in New York in September. Working in Tokyo has been wonderful, but now I need a new challenge.
>
> I think my move is a great chance for you too. I've been very impressed by your work and you have more experience than anyone in the sales team. I hope you'll seriously consider applying for my position. I suggest you update your résumé soon! You can expect my full support.
> Best
>
> Julia

1. Julia's time in Tokyo has been _____.

    A. difficult and unpleasant

    B. really good

    C. fun and easy

2. Julia has been impressed by Takashi's work. This means that Takashi's work has been _____.

    A. getting worse

    B. just average

    C. really good

3. Which statement is correct?

    A. Julia wants Takashi to move to New York.

    B. Julia suggests that Takashi apply for her position.

    C. Julia has already started working in New York.

NOTES

take up: 引き受ける　　résumé: 履歴書

CHALLENGE YOURSELF!

リスニングテストで自分の力を試してみましょう。

Part I • Photographs

A～Cの英文を聞いて写真の描写として最も適切なものを選びましょう。 64

1.

    A   B   C

2.

    A   B   C

Part II • Question-Response

最初に聞こえてくる英文に対する応答として最も適切なものをA～Cの中から選びましょう。 65

3.   A   B   C
4.   A   B   C

Part III • Short Conversations

会話を聞き、下の英文が会話の内容とあっていればT（True）、間違っていればF（False）を○で囲みましょう。 66

5. The man likes the new manager, but the woman does not.   T   F
6. They are interested in customer surveys.   T   F

LET'S READ ALOUD & WRITE! 音読筆写で覚えよう！

授業のまとめとして、今日学習した対話文を3回書き写してしっかり覚えましょう。1度英文を声に出して読んでから書き写すと頭に残りやすくなります。

今日の一言

Experience is the best teacher. （経験は最良の知）

If I were you, I wouldn't miss it.

文法 仮定法

ジュリアが辞めるという話に驚いたタカシでしたが、ある日人事部長のベスに呼び出されます。会話では、用件を尋ねたり、説得したりする表現を学びます。また、文法では**仮定法**に焦点を当てて学習します。

WARM-UP 授業前に確認しておこう！

Vocabulary Preview

1〜10の語句の意味として適切なものをa〜jの中から選びましょう。　CD 67

1. miss	_____	a.	力、強み
2. own	_____	b.	よい機会、好機
3. such	_____	c.	申し出
4. offer	_____	d.	〜のように
5. think over	_____	e.	自身の、独自の
6. leave	_____	f.	〜がいないのをさびしく思う、見逃す
7. opportunity	_____	g.	（会社、仕事などを）辞める、去る
8. energy	_____	h.	元気、気力
9. like	_____	i.	〜をよく考える、熟考する
10. strength	_____	j.	そのような

ビートに乗って1〜10の語句を発音してみましょう。

Grammar Point　仮定法

If you **don't** hurry, you**'ll** be late for the meeting. （急がないと会議に遅れますよ）[直説法]
I don't know the result. If I **knew**, **I'd** tell you.
　　　　（結果は知らないのです。もし知っていたらあなたに話しますよ）[仮定法]

if... は「もし〜ならば」のように条件を表すので **if 節**や**条件節**と言います。この if 節の中で現在のことなのに過去形を使う場合があります。これが**仮定法**と呼ばれるもので、現実と違うことや可能性のないことについて話す場合に使われます。仮定法は、**形は過去でも意味は現在のことを表している**ので注意が必要です。次の例でその違いを確認しましょう。

> 2語以上の単語で1つのまとまった意味を表すもののうち、主語＋述語が含まれているものを**節**、含まれていないものを**句**と言います。

直説法	起こりそうなこと、可能性があること	I**'ll** go to the concert if I **can** get a ticket.
仮定法	現実ではないこと、可能性がないこと	If I **were** you, I **wouldn't** go to the concert.

仮定法には、現在のことを話す**仮定法過去**と、過去のことを話す**仮定法過去完了**があり、基本的な形は次のようになります。

仮定法過去	もし〜なら …だろうに	If ＋主語＋動詞の過去形, 主語＋ would（could, might など）＋動詞の原形 ex.) If I <u>knew</u> Julia's phone number, I <u>would call</u> her now.
仮定法過去完了	もし〜だったら …だっただろうに	If ＋主語＋動詞の過去完了形, 主語＋ would（could, might など）＋ have ＋過去分詞 ex.) If I <u>had known</u> Julia's phone number, I <u>would have called</u> her then.

仮定法では if 節を使ったものがよく知られていますが、if 節がなくても wish に続く節では仮定法が使われ、実現できそうにない願望を示します。また、共に「願う」という意味の wish と hope は使い方が異なりますので、下の例文の日本語訳を完成させながら使い方を確認しましょう。

× I hope you a pleasant stay here.

I'm sorry I have to go. I <u>wish</u> I could stay longer.
(＿＿＿＿＿＿＿＿＿＿＿＿＿＿＿＿＿＿＿＿＿＿＿＿＿＿)

I <u>wish</u> you a pleasant stay here.
(＿＿＿＿＿＿＿＿＿＿＿＿＿＿＿＿＿＿＿＿＿＿＿＿＿＿)

× I wish you enjoy your stay here.

I <u>hope</u> you enjoy your stay here.
(＿＿＿＿＿＿＿＿＿＿＿＿＿＿＿＿＿＿＿＿＿＿＿＿＿＿)

幸運などを祈る場合、wish だと《wish ＋人＋物》、hope だと《hope ＋主語＋動詞》のパターンをとります。
例：I hope you have a pleasant stay here.

LET'S LISTEN! 会話の大意を聞き取ろう！

タカシと人事部長ベスの会話を聞いて、質問に対する答えとして最も適切なものを A〜C の中から１つ選びましょう。 68

Question 1 When did Takashi first hear that Julia would leave the company?

A. Yesterday
B. A few days ago
C. A few weeks ago

Question 2 What does Takashi say about Julia?

A. He doesn't like her.
B. He doesn't know what to say right now.
C. He will miss her a lot.

Question 3 What does Beth tell Takashi?

A. He should give her his answer now.
B. She will miss Julia, too.
C. She wants his answer next week.

LET'S CHECK & READ ALOUD! 音読してみよう！

1. スクリプトを見ながら会話をもう１度聞き、下線部に当てはまる表現を書き入れましょう。（下線部には単語が２つ入ります）
2. 内容を確認して、全文を音読してみましょう。
3. Takashi と Beth の役割をパートナーと一緒に演じてみましょう。

Beth: Hi, Takashi. Thank you for coming. Have a seat.

Takashi: Thank you. What is it that you'd like to discuss?

Beth: Well, did you hear Julia ①_____?

Takashi: Yes, only a few days ago. She's a great manager to work for. I'll ②_____.

Beth: Well, ③_____ you're the best person for her position.

Takashi: Me? But I'm afraid it's too much responsibility for me. I ④_____ like her.

Beth: You don't have to. You have your ⑤_____ and energy. Well, this is a great opportunity for you. If I were you, I ⑥_____ it.

Takashi: This is such a nice offer, but I don't know ⑦_____ say right now.

Beth: Of course, you don't have to decide now. I'll talk to you again next week.

Takashi: I see. I'll think ⑧_____ and get back to you.

音読のヒント

can't や wouldn't など、否定を表す語は一般に強勢を入れて発音します。強勢を入れて発音する場合、ただ声を大きくするのではなく、**強く、はっきりと、長めに**発音します。例えば、can't [kænt] は、「キャァント」といった感じです。反対に、肯定の can は強勢を入れず、**弱く、曖昧に、短く**発音します。[kən]「カン」や [kn]「クン」といった感じです。

GRAMMAR 文法に強くなろう！

A. 例にならい空欄に wish もしくは hope のいずれかを選んで、次の1～4の文を完成させましょう。

例　I (wish) you a merry Christmas.

1. Good-bye. We (　　　　) you luck in your new job.
2. Here's a present for you. I (　　　　) you like it.
3. I'm looking forward to the event and (　　　　) you every success for it.
4. We (　　　　) everything goes well with you.

B. 例にならいカッコ内から正しい語句を選び○で囲みましょう。

例　If it ((rains) / rained) tomorrow, we will cancel the trip.

1. I wish I (have / had) a tablet computer.
2. If you (have / had) any questions, feel free to ask me.
3. I hope this new product (sells / sold) well.
4. I wish I (can / could) help you, but I'm busy now. I'm sorry.

C. 日本語の意味に合うようにカッコ内の語句を並び替え、英文を完成させましょう。

1. 値段が高すぎなければそのチケットを買います。

   I (if / too expensive / it / isn't / will / buy the ticket).

   _____

2. 時間があれば出かけるのですけど。

   I (go out / if / I / had / time / would).

   _____

3. そのホテルはあまりよくありません。私があなただったら泊まりませんよ。

   The hotel isn't very good. I (I / you / wouldn't / were / if / stay there).

   _____

4. もっと早く出発していたら電車に乗り遅れなかっただろうに。

   If I had left earlier, (I / have / train / the / wouldn't / missed).

   _____

LET'S READ!

次のパッセージを読んで１～３の質問に答えましょう。

Working in a Foreign Country

Julia has been working in a foreign country–Japan–for three years. Now it's time for her to spread her wings and fly. Are you the kind of person who would take this kind of opportunity? As you can imagine, working abroad has good and bad points. You'd have a chance to experience new cultures, meet new people, see new ways of doing things, and maybe learn a new language. But you may also miss your family, and the language barrier may cause you to experience cultural stress. It's not a holiday! Think it over. Would you choose to take this opportunity?

1. Julia feels it's time for her to "spread her wings and fly." This suggests that she _____.

    A. enjoys dangerous sports

    B. needs a new challenge

    C. used to be a pilot

2. _____ there are many good points to working abroad, there may be some difficulties too.

    A. Because

    B. Although

    C. As soon as

3. The good points of working abroad include _____.

    A. missing your family

    B. experiencing cultural stress

    C. getting to know new people

NOTES

spread: 広げる　　　abroad: 海外で　　　barrier: 障害

CHALLENGE YOURSELF!

リスニングテストで自分の力を試してみましょう。

Part I • Photographs

A～Cの英文を聞いて写真の描写として最も適切なものを選びましょう。

1.

   A　　B　　C

2.

   A　　B　　C

Part II • Question-Response

最初に聞こえてくる英文に対する応答として最も適切なものをA～Cの中から選びましょう。

3. A　　B　　C
4. A　　B　　C

Part III • Short Conversations

会話を聞き、下の英文が会話の内容とあっていればT（True）、間違っていればF（False）を○で囲みましょう。

5. Takashi needs to work overtime today. 　　　T　　F
6. The woman gives the man a ten percent discount. 　　　T　　F

LET'S READ ALOUD & WRITE! 音読筆写で覚えよう！

授業のまとめとして、今日学習した対話文を3回書き写してしっかり覚えましょう。1度英文を声に出して読んでから書き写すと頭に残りやすくなります。

今日の一言

If there were no clouds, we would not enjoy the sun.
（雲がなければ太陽の喜びはない）

UNIT 15 I'd like to propose a toast.

文法 接続詞・前置詞

ヘッドハンティングされ別の会社へ移ることになったジュリアの送別会でタカシが乾杯の音頭をとります。会話では、感謝の意を示したり、発表したりする表現を学びます。また、文法では**接続詞・前置詞**に焦点を当てて学習します。

WARM-UP 授業前に確認しておこう！

Vocabulary Preview

1〜10の語句の意味として適切なものをa〜jの中から選びましょう。　CD 72

1. attention　_____　　a. よく知られている
2. announce　_____　　b. 分かちあう、共有する
3. past　_____　　c. もう1度
4. share　_____　　d. 注意
5. propose　_____　　e. 祝杯、乾杯
6. take over　_____　　f. 引き継ぐ
7. well-known　_____　　g. 〜を提案する
8. toast　_____　　h. これまでの、過ぎ去った
9. once again　_____　　i. 価値がある
10. worthwhile　_____　　j. 発表する

ビートに乗って1〜10の語句を発音してみましょう。

Grammar Point　接続詞・前置詞

<u>As</u> you may already know, I'm moving to New York.
　　（すでにご存じかもしれませんが、私はニューヨークに引っ越します）［接続詞］
I think I can do a good job <u>as</u> your assistant.
　　（私は助手としてよい仕事ができると思います）［前置詞］
Did you quit <u>because of</u> your boss?　（上司のせいで仕事を辞めたのかい？）［前置詞］
Julia was angry <u>because</u> I didn't contact her sooner.
　　（私がもっと早く連絡しなかったのでジュリアは腹を立てていた）［接続詞］

接続詞は様々な語や句、節などを結びつける役割を果たすものです。and や if のようによく知られたものの他、every time（〜する度に）や in case（〜の場合は）などのように2語以上で接続詞的に使われるものもあります。次の表に枠の中から適切な接続詞を書き入れて確認しましょう。

because	～なので	after	～した後で	unless	～しなければ	unless ✓
or	または	before	～する前に		～だけれども	so
	それで	when	～するとき	as soon as	～したらすぐに	although
						until
while	～の間		～するまで		～である限りは	as long as

次に、**前置詞**は、<u>in</u> June や <u>on</u> the desk のように、**名詞や名詞句の前に置かれ、形容詞や副詞の役割を果たすもの**です。前置詞と名詞が一緒になったものを**前置詞句**と呼びます。

接続詞と前置詞では、while と during、because と because of など、意味の似たものがありますので違いを確認しておきましょう。接続詞と前置詞を見分けるポイントは右の表の通りです。

接続詞	その後に主語と動詞を含む語句（＝節）が続く。 ex.) Kate canceled her trip **because** she was ill.
前置詞	その後に主語と動詞を含まない語句（＝句）が続く。 ex.) Kate canceled her trip **because of** her illness.

下の例文の日本語訳を完成させながら使い方を確認しましょう。

Don't call me at work <u>unless</u> it's an emergency.
　（緊急事態 _____ ）

We're open from 10 a.m. to 6 p.m. <u>during</u> the week, and 10 a.m. to 8 p.m. on weekends.
　（当店は _____ ）

There was a phone call for you <u>while</u> you were out.
　（ _____ ）

LET'S LISTEN!　会話の大意を聞き取ろう！

タカシとジュリアのスピーチを聞いて、質問に対する答えとして最も適切なものを
A～Cの中から1つ選びましょう。

Question 1　What is Julia's next job?

　A. President of a marketing company
　B. Vice president of a marketing company
　C. Vice president of a design company

Question 2　What does Julia say about her three years in Japan?

　A. Useful
　B. Long
　C. Surprising

Question 3　What are they probably going to do next?

　A. Drink to their future
　B. Make a speech
　C. Say goodbye to each other

LET'S CHECK & READ ALOUD! 音読してみよう！

1. スクリプトを見ながら会話をもう1度聞き、下線部に当てはまる表現を書き入れましょう。（下線部には単語が2つ入ります）
2. 内容を確認して、全文を音読してみましょう。
3. Takashi と Julia の役割をパートナーと一緒に演じてみましょう。

Takashi: Could I have your attention, please? ①_____ know, this party is to say goodbye to Julia. ②_____ a great job as our leader and we've learned a lot from her. ③_____ to New York as vice president of a well-known marketing company. So I'd like ④_____ a toast to Julia. Congratulations and good luck! Cheers!

Julia: Thank you very much. The ⑤_____ years have been truly worthwhile. I've enjoyed working in Japan and, of course, working with you all. I'll miss all of you very much. Also, I'd like to ⑥_____ you some great news. I'm pleased to ⑦_____ Takashi is taking over my job as the new sales manager. So I'd like to propose a toast once again. To your new manager and to a ⑧_____ for all of us.

DID YOU KNOW?

会話の中で出てきた "Congratulations!" は、「おめでとう！」と相手を祝福する際によく使われるものですが、必ず複数形で使うことに注意しましょう。また、この言葉は結婚した新郎にも使われますが、本来努力して何かを成し遂げた人に対して使われるものですから、クリスマスや正月などのときの挨拶には使われません。

GRAMMAR 文法に強くなろう！

A. 例にならい枠の中から適切な語句を選んで次の1〜4の文を完成させましょう。必要な場合は適切な形に変化させましょう。

   例　This is a secret between you (*and*) me, OK?

   1. It doesn't matter (　　　　) you like his idea or not.
   2. I was very tired, (　　　　) I went to bed early.
   3. I'll let you know (　　　　) a decision is made.
   4. (　　　　) Julia can speak Japanese, she can't write it.

   whether
   so
   although
   as soon as
   and ✓

B. 例にならいカッコ内から正しい語句を選び○で囲みましょう。

   例　We left the office ((at) / on) seven o'clock.

   1. Julia canceled the meeting (because / because of) her illness.
   2. I will finish this sales report (by / until) five o'clock.
   3. The meeting is tomorrow. Can you finish the report (for / in) a day?
   4. We talked about the project (during / while) lunch break.

C. 日本語の意味に合うようにカッコ内の語句を並び替え、英文を完成させましょう。ただし、文の始めにくる単語も小文字にしてあります。

   1. お願いがあるのですが。
      I was wondering (a favor / I / you / could / ask / if).

   2. 会議は8月1日の午後に201号室で開かれます。
      The meeting (on / be / Room 201 / held / will / in) the afternoon of August 1.

   3. 私にできることがあればお知らせください。
      (anything / can / I / there / is / if) do for you, please let me know.

   4. あなたのいけないところはすぐに諦めてしまうことです。
      (you / is / the / with / that / trouble) you give up easily.

LET'S READ!

次のパッセージを読んで1～3の質問に答えましょう。

A Good Career Move

Julia is an ambitious person. She wants to work hard and be successful. In her latest career move, she's going to New York. She'll have more responsibility and maybe also a better salary.

Are you ambitious? Is success in your work important to you? When you start job-hunting, you'll need to make some choices about your future. Would you rather work for a big company, a small one, or be self-employed? Would you like a lot of responsibility, or would you prefer a quiet life? Why not ask your partner about their future career plans?

1. An ambitious person is someone who wants to _____.

    A. stay at home

    B. do really well in their career

    C. enjoy a quiet family life

2. The underlined "career move" is a change that you make _____.

    A. to get a better job

    B. to start your own business

    C. to live and work in a new town

3. People who are "self-employed" work for _____.

    A. a selfish employer

    B. a very low salary

    C. themselves, in their own company or business

NOTES

salary: 給料   job-hunting: 就職活動

CHALLENGE YOURSELF!

リスニングテストで自分の力を試してみましょう。

Part I • Photographs

A～Cの英文を聞いて写真の描写として最も適切なものを選びましょう。

1. A B C

2. A B C

Part II • Question-Response

最初に聞こえてくる英文に対する応答として最も適切なものをA～Cの中から選びましょう。

3. A B C
4. A B C

Part III • Short Conversations

会話を聞き、下の英文が会話の内容とあっていればT（True）、間違っていればF（False）を〇で囲みましょう。

5. The woman says that she can finish the report by Friday.　　T　F
6. The 11 o'clock ferry to Dover is delayed due to engine trouble.　　T　F

LET'S READ ALOUD & WRITE! 音読筆写で覚えよう！

授業のまとめとして、今日学習した対話文を3回書き写してしっかり覚えましょう。1度英文を声に出して読んでから書き写すと頭に残りやすくなります。

今日の一言

Look before you leap.（石橋を叩いて渡る／転ばぬ先の杖）

巻末資料

品詞の分類

名詞や動詞といった文法上の区分のことを**品詞**と言い、一般に下のように分類されます。

品詞	働き	例
名詞（Noun）	人や物事の名前を表す。	company, sale など
冠詞（Article）	名詞の前に置かれて、その単語が特定されるものかどうかを示す。	a, an, the
代名詞（Pronoun）	名詞の代わりをする。	I, my, me, mine など
動詞（Verb）	人や物事の状態や動作を表す。	want, keep, take など
助動詞（Auxiliary verb）	動詞と組み合わせて話し手の判断を示す。	can, will, must など
形容詞（Adjective）	人や物事の性質や状態などを表す。	big, beautiful など
副詞（Adverb）	動詞や形容詞などを修飾する。	really, always など
前置詞（Preposition）	名詞や名詞句の前に置かれ句を作る。	of, in, under, on など
接続詞（Conjunction）	語と語、句と句、節と節をつなぐ。	and, because, or など
間投詞（Interjection）	話し手の感情を表す。	oh, wow, ouch など

単語は必ずしも1つの品詞でしか使われないわけではありません。意味のわからない単語を辞書で引く場合も、その単語の品詞が何であるかをあらかじめ考えておくと、正しい意味に早くたどり着けるようになります。

文の要素と基本文型

英文を構成する要素には次のようなものがあります。

主語	文の中で「〜が、〜は」に当たるもの。	名詞、代名詞
述語動詞	文の中で「〜である」や「〜する」に当たるもの。	動詞
目的語	「〜を」や「〜に」など、動作の対象を示すもの。	名詞、代名詞
補語	主語や目的語が「どういうものか」もしくは「どんな状態なのか」を補足説明するもの。 ex）My name is Robert, but everybody calls me Bob. （私の名前はロバートですが、みんな私のことをボブと呼びます）	名詞、代名詞、形容詞
修飾語（句）	主語、述語動詞、目的語、補語に意味を付け加えるもの。 修飾語（句）を除いても文は成立します。 ex）I work for Sunrise Corporation. （私はサンライズ・コーポレーションに勤めています）	形容詞、副詞、前置詞句など

また、英文の基本文型としては下に挙げる **5 文型**がよく知られています。

第 1 文型	SV（主語＋動詞）	I cried. （私は泣いた）
第 2 文型	SVC（主語＋動詞＋補語）	My name is Robert. （私の名前はロバートです）
第 3 文型	SVO（主語＋動詞＋目的語）	I studied economics. （私は経済学を学びました）
第 4 文型	SVO_1O_2（主語＋動詞＋目的語＋目的語）	Julia gave me the report. （ジュリアが私にその報告書をくれました）
第 5 文型	SVOC（主語＋動詞＋目的語＋補語）	Everybody calls me Bob. （みんな私のことをボブと呼びます）

主語（Subject）、**述語動詞**（Verb）、**目的語**（Object）、**補語**（Complement）という基本要素の中で、目的語と補語の区別が文型を見分けるポイントになります。目的語は動詞が表す動作の対象を示し、補語は主語や目的語が「どういうものか」もしくは「どんな状態なのか」を補足説明するものです。ですから、第 2 文型と第 3 文型を見分ける場合、「**第 2 文型の場合 S ＝ C、第 3 文型の場合 S ≠ O**」という関係に着目するとよいでしょう。また、第 4 文型と第 5 文型を見分ける場合には、「**第 4 文型の場合 O_1 ≠ O_2、第 5 文型の場合 O ＝ C**」という関係が成り立つことに注意しておくことです。

人称代名詞の種類と格変化表

人 称	数	主格 （～は）	所有格 （～の）	目的格 （～に、～を）	所有代名詞 （～のもの）	再帰代名詞 （～自身）
1 人称	単数	I	my	me	mine	myself
	複数	we	our	us	ours	ourselves
2 人称	単数	you	your	you	yours	yourself
	複数					yourselves
3 人称	単数	he	his	him	his	himself
		she	her	her	hers	herself
		it	its	it	─	itself
	複数	they	their	them	theirs	themselves

音 節

音節とは、簡単に言うと、「母音を中心とした音のかたまり」で、[ái] といった二重母音も 1 つの母音と考えます。hot [hát] や big [bíg] などのごく短い単語は 1 音節ですが、strike [stráik] など、一見長そうに見える単語でも母音は [ái] しかありませんので、実は 1 音節です。

単語が何音節であるかは、辞書に載っています。例えば、interesting を辞書で調べてみると、in・ter・est・ing のように区切られて表示されており、この区切りが音節の区切りを示しています。したがって、interesting は 4 音節だとわかります。

慣れるまでは辞書で確かめるようにしてください。

不規則動詞変化表

	原形	過去形	過去分詞形	-ing 形	
A-A-A （原形、過去形、過去分詞がすべて同じ）	cost cut hit put read	cost cut hit put read [réd]	cost cut hit put read [réd]	costing cutting hitting putting reading	（費用が）かかる 切る 叩く 置く 読む
A-B-A （原形と過去分詞が同じ）	become come run	became came ran	become come run	becoming coming running	〜になる 来る 走る
A-B-B （過去形と過去分詞が同じ）	bring buy catch feel have hear keep leave make meet pay say spend stand teach tell think understand	brought bought caught felt had heard kept left made met paid said spent stood taught told thought understood	brought bought caught felt had heard kept left made met paid said spent stood taught told thought understood	bringing buying catching feeling having hearing keeping leaving making meeting paying saying spending standing teaching telling thinking understanding	持ってくる 買う 捕まえる 感じる 持っている 聞く 保つ 立ち去る 作る 会う 払う 言う 過ごす 立つ 教える 話す 思う 理解する
A-B-C （原形、過去形、過去分詞がすべて異なる）	be begin break choose drink eat fall get give go know see speak take write	was / were began broke chose drank ate fell got gave went knew saw spoke took wrote	been begun broken chosen drunk eaten fallen gotten/got given gone known seen spoken taken written	being beginning breaking choosing drinking eating falling getting giving going knowing seeing speaking taking writing	〜である 始まる 壊す 選ぶ 飲む 食べる 落ちる 手に入れる 与える 行く 知っている 見る 話す 取る 書く

発音記号の読み方① 母音編

■母音と子音
「母音」とは、日本語の「アイウエオ」のように、肺から出る空気が舌や歯、唇などに邪魔されずに自由に口から出る音のことです。これに対して、「子音」とは、喉から出る息や声が途中でいろいろと邪魔されて、口や鼻から出る音のことです。

■有声音と無声音
声帯が振動する音のことを「有声音」と言い、逆に声帯が振動しない音のことを「無声音」と言います。母音はすべて有声音ですが、子音には有声音と無声音の両方があります。

 77, 78

短母音	[ɑ]	口を思いきり開け口の奥の方から「ア」。	box / hot
	[ʌ]	口をあまり開けない「ア」。	come / bus
	[ə]	口を軽く開けて弱く「ア」。	woman / about
	[æ]	「エ」の口の形で「ア」。	bank / hand
	[i]	日本語の「イ」と「エ」の中間。	sick / it
	[i:]	唇を左右に引いて「イー」。	see / chief
	[u]	[u:]よりも少し唇をゆるめて「ウ」	good / look
	[u:]	唇を小さく丸めて「ウー」。	school / two
	[e]	日本語の「エ」とほぼ同じ。	net / desk
	[ɔ:]	口を大きく開け唇を少し丸めて「オー」。	talk / ball
	[a:r]	口を大きく開けて「アー」の後、舌先を巻き上げた音を添える。	large / far
	[ə:r]	口を軽く開けて「アー」の後、舌先を巻き上げた音を添える。	girl / work
二重母音	[ei]	始めの音を強く発音し、後の音は軽く添える感じで、「エィ」。	game / say
	[ɔi]	上と同じ感じで、「オィ」。	boy / oil
	[ai]	上と同じ感じで、「アィ」。	write / kind
	[au]	上と同じ感じで、「アゥ」。	house / now
	[ou]	上と同じ感じで、「オゥ」。	boat / cold
	[iər]	「イァ」に舌先を巻き上げた音を添える。	dear / hear
	[eər]	「エァ」に舌先を巻き上げた音を添える。	air / bear
	[uər]	「ウァ」に舌先を巻き上げた音を添える。	poor / tour

発音記号の読み方② 子音編

 79～84

破裂音	[p]	「パ」行子音とほぼ同じ。	pen / cup
	[b]	[p]の有声音。「バ」行子音とほぼ同じ。	big / job
	[t]	「タ」行子音とほぼ同じ。	tea / meet
	[d]	[t]の有声音。「ダ」行子音とほぼ同じ。	day / food
	[k]	「カ」行子音とほぼ同じ。	cook / take
	[g]	[k]の有声音。「ガ」行子音とほぼ同じ。	game / leg
摩擦音	[f]	下唇を上の歯にあて、息を出して「フ」。	five / enough
	[v]	[f]の有声音で、「ヴ」。	voice / wave
	[θ]	舌先を前歯で軽く噛むようにして「ス」。	think / month
	[ð]	[θ]の有声音で、「ズ」。	there / brother
	[s]	「サ、ス、セ、ソ」の子音とほぼ同じ。	sea / nice
	[z]	[s]の有声音で、「ザ、ズ、ゼ、ゾ」の子音とほぼ同じ。	zoo / lose
	[ʃ]	「シ」とほぼ同じ。	she / fish
	[ʒ]	[ʃ]の有声音で、「ジ」。	usual / vision
	[h]	「ハー」と息を吹きかけてガラスを曇らせるときのような「ハ」。	hot / hand
破擦音	[tʃ]	「チャ」「チュ」「チョ」の子音とほぼ同じ。	church / watch
	[dʒ]	[tʃ]の有声音で、「ヂャ」「ヂュ」「ヂョ」の子音とほぼ同じ。	join / edge
鼻音	[m]	「マ」行子音とほぼ同じ。	meet / time
	[n]	舌の先を上の歯茎につけて、鼻から息を出す。	noon / run
	[ŋ]	[g]を言うつもりで、鼻から声を出す。	thing / song
側音	[l]	必ず舌の先を上の歯茎につける。	late / wall
移行音	[r]	「ウ」のように唇をすぼめる感じで、舌先は歯茎に決してつけない。	red / marry
	[w]	唇をよく丸めて発音する。	way / quick
	[j]	「ヤ、ユ、ヨ」の子音とほぼ同じ。	young / beyond

LINGUAPORTA

リンガポルタのご案内

リンガポルタ連動テキストをご購入の学生さんは、「リンガポルタ」を無料でご利用いただけます！

　本テキストで学習していただく内容に準拠した問題を、オンライン学習システム「リンガポルタ」で学習していただくことができます。PCだけでなく、スマートフォンやタブレットでも学習できます。単語や文法、リスニング力などをよりしっかり身に付けていただくため、ぜひ積極的に活用してください。

　リンガポルタの利用にはアカウントとアクセスコードの登録が必要です。登録方法については下記ページにアクセスしてください。

https://www.seibido.co.jp/linguaporta/register.html

本テキスト「Let's Read Aloud More!」のアクセスコードは下記です。

4786-2043-1231-0365-0003-005e-LCCF-FB46

・リンガポルタの学習機能（画像はサンプルです。また、すべてのテキストに以下の4つの機能が用意されているわけではありません）

● 多肢選択

● 空所補充（音声を使っての聞き取り問題も可能）

● 単語並びかえ（マウスや手で単語を移動）

● マッチング（マウスや手で単語を移動）

TEXT PRODUCTION STAFF

edited by	編集	
Takashi Kudo	工藤 隆志	
cover design by	表紙デザイン	
Ruben Frosali	ルーベン・フロサリ	
text design by	本文デザイン	
Miyuki Inde	印出 美由紀	
illustration by	イラスト	
Yoko Sekine	関根 庸子	

CD PRODUCTION STAFF

recorded by	吹き込み者
Edith Kayumi (AmE)	イーディス・カユミ（アメリカ英語）
Jack Merluzzi (AmE)	ジャック・マルージ（アメリカ英語）

Let's Read Aloud More!
音読で極める基礎英語

2015年12月27日 初 版 発 行
2022年 5 月20日 第9刷 発 行

著　者　　角山 照彦　　Simon Capper
発行者　　佐野 英一郎
発行所　　株式会社 成美堂
　　　　　〒101-0052　東京都千代田区神田小川町3-22
　　　　　TEL 03-3291-2261　FAX 03-3293-5490
　　　　　https://www.seibido.co.jp

印刷・製本　　三美印刷(株)

ISBN 978-4-7919-4786-7　　　　　　　　　　　　　Printed in Japan

・落丁・乱丁本はお取り替えします。
・本書の無断複写は、著作権上の例外を除き著作権侵害となります。